Postcards
to Europe

WEIDENFELD & NICOLSON

First published in Great Britain in 2017 as *Goodbye Europe*
This paperback edition first published in 2019 by Weidenfeld & Nicolson
an imprint of The Orion Publishing Group Ltd
Carmelite House, 50 Victoria Embankment
London EC4Y 0DZ

An Hachette UK Company

1 3 5 7 9 10 8 6 4 2

www.orionbooks.co.uk

Contents

DOUBLE RAINBOW

Richard Herring

RICHARD HERRING is an award-winning English stand-up comedian, comedy writer, podcaster, playwright and diarist. He is the author of *Fist of Fun* (with Stewart Lee), *Talking Cock*, *Warming Up Volume I: Bye Bye Balham*, *How Not To Grow Up*, *Warming Up Volume II: The Box Lady and Other Pesticles*, and *Emergency Questions*.

It's amazing we managed to stay together for so long. Great Britain was like a puerile younger sibling to the cool, sexually confident, cigarette smoking teenager of the Continent. We must have been an embarrassment when we turned up sniggering at *double entendres* while you were trying to party with your sophisticated peers. And yet you cared enough to forgive us our immaturity and try to guide us towards a future where we finally grew up.

But we threw our toys out of our pram because we couldn't accept that the world didn't revolve around us.

Here's a story that summed up the difference between us. I should have known we were bound to break up. I was on a skiing holiday in Austria with my wife and daughter. I didn't want to go skiing, I had never done it before and I knew I'd be terrible at it, and I was correct. It was horrific.

Firstly you put on boots that are so tight that every movement you make for the rest of the day is like being tortured on a rack. Then you are transported up a mountain, which you are expected to slide down on some sticks. You fall over, you might ski off a cliff, there could be avalanches and it's freezing cold. The only good thing about the whole experience is when you get to the end of the day and take the boots off. It's

3

just such a beautiful release to no longer be in constant agony that it almost induces euphoria. I wanted to shout, 'Thank you for freeing me! You have made me appreciate how wonderful my life is. I will never complain about anything again.'

On the final day of the vacation I told my wife I wasn't going back. She was fine with that. The hotel had a luxury spa and she wanted to go for a sauna. I can't understand the pleasure in this either. You go into a tiny wooden box which is unbearably hot and it's impossible to breathe, which is how it must feel to be buried alive. I just want to go on a holiday where I am a normal temperature. Is that too much to ask?

My wife wanted to look round the spa, so she told me to meet her in the sauna. I have been married long enough to know that I must do as I am told. I went into the leisure-tomb wearing my swimming trunks. I am a normal English man and would never have considered wearing anything else.

Thirty seconds later the door opened. I thought my wife would enter, but instead a European lady of about fifty-five years of age walked in. The thing I noticed about her immediately was that she was completely naked: no swimming costume, no underwear. She didn't ask my permission to disrobe she just waltzed in, smiling at me and saying 'Hello!', as if being naked was the most natural thing in the world.

Then she lay down opposite me with her bottom bits smiling up at me, like some kind of end-to-end flesh-coloured double rainbow. I didn't know where not to look. I'd have gone red and had steam coming out of my ears, if I hadn't been in a sauna so that was already happening.

Then my wife came through the door. What was she going to say? She'd only been gone a minute and here I was in a compromising position with a mature European. But my wife recognised that this was something sophisticated and Continental, and being one-eighth Norwegian wanted to appear sophisticated as well, so she acted as if nothing out of the ordinary was going on. But there is nothing sophisticated about not sniggering like a schoolchild when presented with an unexpected noo-noo. You could see this lady's chuff. The whole thing. I'm guessing. I wasn't staring at it. But it was hard to avoid. It followed you round the room. It was like the eye of Sauron.

I was forty-eight at the time and perhaps I should have been able to take a stranger's tuppence in my stride. But I am British and embarrassed enough by my own raddled genitalia. I wouldn't foist that on a stranger and I felt awkward that someone had presumed to show me theirs. I had to leave. Out of embarrassment. Are you seeing why I am making this analogy?

It was only once I was out of the sauna that I saw there was a sign saying it was hotel policy that you HAD to be naked in the sauna. The rules had been clearly displayed all along, but I had failed to notice them ... After all this it was I who had committed the social faux pas by hiding my pocket-rocket away. The lady must have thought I was so rude – why wasn't I swinging my penis round like a helicopter? What had she done to offend me.

It also said that anyone under fourteen wasn't allowed into the sauna. Thank God. But that meant anyone fourteen or over WAS allowed in the sauna. I'd been mentally scarred by this as a man of nearly fifty, imagine if the fourteen-year-old Richard Herring had been in there. The only vagina I'd seen at that point had been in a torn-up copy of *Fiesta* that I'd found in Shipham woods. And I had nightmares about that for twenty-three years.

I voted Brexit because of this. We don't want to be a part of that. We're better off without the Europeans if that's their concept of normality!

To be fair, that's no more ridiculous than the reasons that anyone else voted for Brexit. It's pretty much the only one that still stands up. They should have put that on the side of a bus. That woman's nether regions looking down on us all, saying 'Is this what you want?'

Our repressed nation isn't ready to hang out with you Gauloise smoking Europeans. I hope, in a few more years, we might be.

WHY THE FIGHT
IS SO BITTER

Alain de Botton

The debate about whether and how the UK should leave the European Union should be one of the most boring of all in politics, involving as it does arcane discussions around tariffs, import duties, rebates, fishing quotas for mackerel and the rights of banks to sell eurobonds across national borders. This should be the sort of stuff of which the unread back business pages of newspapers are made.

Instead, the debate on Europe has become – in the UK at least – an issue which divides families, splits couples, destroys friendships and strikes at the heart of personal and emotional life. People are going into psychotherapy with the presenting problems simply being: Brexit.

How has an issue around the minutiae of trading rules become an issue over which people define their identities and determine their personal lives?

Because leaving the EU isn't primarily a political or even economic matter. It is first and foremost a cultural one, by which is meant, a debate about what sort of people the British should be, what sort of values they should live by, what they should hold dear and, quite simply, how they should live.

Beneath the technocratic arguments of Brexit stir two competing cultural visions of Europe and two related competing cultural visions of England (it's best at this point simply to speak of England, for Brexit is above anything else a crisis within the soul of England, not that of Wales, Scotland or Northern Ireland).

Those who argue over 'Europe' are tussling over what could be summed up as a 'Good Europe' and a 'Bad Europe', loose but meaningful collections of images and moral-ethical-aesthetic positions.

To those who love it, 'Good Europe' means: a social democratic model that mixes respect for the market with high levels of welfare; progressive taxation; trams and trains; a cosmopolitanism of the mind; cafes; a high regard for elite culture; a love of the new and the futuristic; relationships between people of different countries; a suspicion of certain aspects of the United States; holidays by the sea; (and to get a little more fanciful) Modernist architecture; sex; olive trees; and clean clear signage in Helvetica font.

To those who hate it, 'Bad Europe' means: a threat to a prized and superior local historical identity; supranational bossiness; people telling you what to do (in the workplace, in relationships or at the level of the state); dull bureaucracy; French arrogance; German arrogance; continentals who make one feel uncouth and boorish; fancy food that humiliates; immigrants who look odd and speak strangely and are bad neighbours; litter; graffiti; ugly enormous cities full of vagrants and beggars; unsupervised chaos; annoying sexy carefree people; the future; puzzlingly different languages.

But these two coagulations of stereotypes only have an emotional pull because they are the shadows of two competing visions of England. When people squabble over 'Europe' in the UK, what they are really arguing about is what sort of country they should be living in.

Those who love 'Europe' do so essentially because they are in flight from the spectre of a 'Bad England'. 'Bad England' looks a bit like this: parochial rural life; village fetes; ruddy-faced men who wear purple or red trousers; advocates of hunting and shooting; public schools; dumb aristocrats; boarding schools; shepherd's pie (and all it stands for); rainy holidays; apple crumble; greyness; people who hate the future and technology; a lack of sex and glamour; a lack of social ease and sophistication; port wine; Sunday evenings in damp February; joylessness; Stilton.

Conversely, those who hate 'Europe' do so because they feel they are fighting for a 'Good England'. 'Good England' looks a bit like this: the way things always used to be; modesty; fitting in; doing it your own way; who we were in the Second World War; apple crumble; a bit of rain; test cricket on TV; restrained dignity around emotions; knowing how to take a joke; good chaps; not whingeing; wellies; going for a walk; an extra jumper indoors in winter; standing up for yourself; pale legs; unshowy sex; not bothering too much about one's hair or clothes; Stilton.

These categorisations sound, of course, a little daft. That doesn't mean to say they aren't in some way very real inside every British person who finds themselves feeling very intensely about Brexit.

When one goes beneath the surface politics and economics and asks why someone dislikes or admires 'Europe', there will always be a catalytic personal story of some kind, either caused by images of Europe or to which images of Europe are invoked as a solution. 'Good Europe' might be a defence against a bullying father; a childhood in a town one hated; a lack of sex in adolescence; people one hated at school . . . 'Bad Europe' might have begun with one's father's unemployment; a sense of humiliation on a trip abroad; a feeling of being disrespected by elites; an impression of sexual discomfort.

Knowing there are personal fears and aspirations beneath the debates won't neutralise the passion on either side, but it will make for more interesting and authentic conversations. We may start to understand and even sympathise with those who had merely been the enemy. To learn to live with one another once more, the British need to ask odd-sounding questions around the kitchen table: 'How has Europe scared you?' 'How has England traumatised you?' 'To what problem is your imaginary Europe or England the solution?'

We need to stop speaking about the debate on Europe as if it's simply about economics and politics. It's about values and the symbols that carry them: it's about Stilton vs Brie; about pubs vs cafes; about cars vs trams. It's about what we're scared of and what can comfort us. We aren't wrong to be so exercised about 'Europe'. We're wrong to keep discussing the debate in the sober impersonal terms we currently employ.

MA VLAST

Sarah Perry

SARAH PERRY is the author of *The Essex Serpent* and *After Me Comes the Flood*. She has written for numerous publications including the *Guardian*, the *Observer* and the *Financial Times*, and her work has been broadcast on BBC Radio 4 and on RTE1. She has been writer-in-residence at Gladstone's Library and the UNESCO Prague City of Literature writer-in-residence. She lives in Norwich, and is a European.

I'm something of a thief, I'm afraid, and among my stolen possessions I have the score to 'Vltava', the river theme from the Czech composer Smetana's symphonic poem *Ma Vlast* (it means: 'my country'). This I took from school, having played the piano part in the orchestra – nobody, it seemed to me, could possibly love it as I loved it, or play it as I played it; therefore in spirit if not in law it belonged to me.

The Vltava, I knew, is the river that runs through Prague. But I'd never been deeper into Europe, or for any greater length, than a school day-trip to Calais; so Prague was little more to me than a romantic abstraction in which dark-haired women drank coffee from thimble-sized cups at tables where smoke rose from green glass ashtrays, bickering elegantly over politics and men. I recall practising on the piano in the dining room at home, drifting on its minor triplets: it was the current on which I floated out of the Essex town where I was born, across the muddy Channel, into some network of rivers which in due course would wash me up on the banks of the Vltava itself.

Rivers in particular seemed to me an impossibly romantic feature of mainland Europe: my geography was (and remains) inaccurate to the point of idiocy, but I knew how the Danube, for example, began in Germany, and washed through ten countries before emptying itself into Russia's Black Sea. The Severn's modest journey from Wales to Gloucestershire seemed inconsequential in comparison: in Europe, where country abutted country like the pieces of a puzzle, one body of water took in a dozen ways of speaking, a dozen means of baking bread; many hundred ways of telling tales to frighten children when the nights drew in, and of singing in a harvest.

My conception of Europe then was hazy, informed on the one hand by the completion of E111 forms before I took the ferry to Calais, and on the other by the mistrust and contempt with which it was met in the deeply conservative chapel where my family worshipped. I knew that were I to break my leg in the *supermarché* where I exchanged francs for Brie, I would not have to pay to have it set; this seemed to me a sensible arrangement, and an improvement on Harfleur, Passchendaele and Dunkirk. All the same, I was faintly aware the EU was regarded in certain quarters as an invading force massed fifty yards south-east of Dover's white cliffs, its fleet packed to the gunnels with straight bananas, legislation regarding the proper refrigeration of the annual chapel tea and machinery with which to dismantle Parliament. From the Ebenezer pulpit preachers preached, with scripture texts appended, that the EU – in common with the Roman Catholic Church – was foretold in the book of Revelation. The Whore of Babylon was mentioned, though it was never clear whether she was a greater or lesser threat to English sovereignty than a banana more linear than creation intended.

But I was European – we all were – this much I knew. The Christmas tree pulled down the attic hatch each year was

European; the dusty sweet slices of stollen we ate were European; 'Silent Night' was European. Romeo and Juliet were European. So was my father's car. Parliament occasionally lapsed into Norman French; the Essex soil with its crop of sugar beet was sowed with Roman coin. Italy, France, Germany, Spain: I felt a kinship with them which was nothing like the awed and alienated sensation I felt when reading Arundhati Roy, or buying blue plaster scarabs from the British Museum shop.

In 2016 I saw the Vltava for the first time. It was January, and I'd pitched up in Prague for two months on a UNESCO City of Literature residency. My flat overlooked the river through one broad window with a narrow ledge, and here I leaned out into air which was cold in a sweet, sharp way, nothing like the wet chill of an East Anglian winter, watching swans fly downriver through a snowfall. I propped my laptop on the ledge and sent Smetana tinnily out into the city, tapping out the melody with my right hand.

The love I have for Prague is as unearned as it was immediate. I've no right to it: no family connection, no facility with the Czech language or any other, no understanding beyond the cursory of the history of its changing borders; but the kinship I felt when I flatly refused to return that piano score was there from the moment I first walked over Charles Bridge. The stone apostles, the jackdaws, the violinist with his case open for coins; the beggar who corrected my pronunciation of *Jak se máš* ('Good morning') and let me give a biscuit to the dog wrapped in his coat; Master Jan Hus's statue in the Old Town Square, and the good black coffee served with cakes very nearly like those I baked at home, but also nothing like at all: these seemed, in some obscure indefensible way, to belong to me. In cafes I drank coffee from cups small as thimbles; tapped my cigarette into green glass ashtrays; bickered, as elegantly as I could, about politics and men. I wondered if the teenage thief at the piano had known I would one day come. It did not seem impossible: this was *ma vlast*.

Now I am forced out of my hazy, romantic European identity – of that abstract sense of fraternity I never needed to explain or to defend. My conversation turns like gossip to the Single Market, Freedom of Movement, the European Court of Human Rights; I fret about the UK border with Ireland, the Erasmus programme, the Customs Union. But when I think of the night of 23 June 2016, and of what has come after – when I threaten, only half in jest, that on my deathbed I'll recite the name of every family member who voted to take my citizenship from me – it is never in terms of legislation, or of white papers put before Parliament. I think instead of a river that runs from where I stand to the Vltava being dammed up with fistfuls of British soil and scraps of whatever comes to hand; and they're nothing, these fragments – you couldn't build a hut on their foundations – and singly they amount to nothing, but taken together they'll leave me on dry land.

This is a little foolish, of course. The jackdaws, the Vltava, Master Jan Hus: when flights depart Stansted they will be waiting, as they always were. But something has altered. They wait politely now, with good manners, as one waits for a house guest whose stay will be mercifully brief – not with that easeful, familiar welcome reserved for family. The Czech for 'their country' is *jejich vlast*. I cannot pronounce it.

THE TWO STEPHANES

Matt Haig

MATT HAIG is the number one bestselling author of *Reasons to Stay Alive* and *How to Stop Time*. He has also written five highly acclaimed novels for adults, including *The Radleys* and *The Humans*. As a writer for children and young adults he has won the Blue Peter Book Award, the Smarties Book Prize and been shortlisted three times for the Carnegie Medal. His work has been translated into over thirty languages. @matthaig1

My penfriend Stephane lived in a northern suburb of Paris, about twenty miles from the centre. I liked Stephane a lot. He was slightly older than me, slightly stronger, slightly sportier. Golden-haired and happy and tough. I liked his family a lot too. The first time I stayed at their house, when I was eleven or twelve years old, I was sick on their carpet. That first time my parents had been there too and we had greedily devoured the meal of scallops in a creamy wine sauce – coquilles St Jacques – that they had served us. About two hours later I was in the attic bedroom on a sofa bed.

'Mum,' I said, as she had come to say goodnight. 'I feel sick.'

'It's probably homesickness.'

'No. I think it's sickness sickness.'

'Don't be silly, Matthew. Please don't make a scene.'

'Okay. But . . .'

Another ten minutes and it was too late. Too late, and all over their immaculate carpet.

Anyway, the family were ever so nice about it. And a few evenings later, after my parents had left, we went into Paris. I had been to Paris before. But this was totally different. This time I was *driving* in, and in an actual French person's car. I can still picture Stephane's father – who spoke even less English than Stephane – pointing at the landmarks as we drove past them. He even did a little Quasimodo impression as we drove past an illuminated Notre Dame.

I don't think we actually got out of the car that night but it was still one of the most amazing evenings of my entire childhood. To be there, in a foreign city, in a foreign car, with a foreign family: that was the first time it made sense to me. French people were real people. I mean, I obviously always knew they were real people but to actually *know it*. That they were real and ordinary and had family squabbles and went to the toilet. To actually know they were the same as me and my family. With a car and a dog and a loveable but slightly embarrassing dad.

I think the biggest revelation was the fact that they went to McDonald's. I loved telling my parents this. You see, I was banned from going to McDonald's. McDonald's was, as far as my parents were concerned, the seventh circle of Hell. The opposite of what my parents thought I should be eating. What they thought I, or anyone, should be eating was – ideally – French food. Snails, coq au vin, or maybe just some Brie. Not that we ever actually ate much of that sort of stuff, except the Brie, which I was always a little suspicious of, but French food in late 1980s England, or at least in our house, was seen as the height of sophistication, even if it wasn't actually eaten that much. My mum had been an au pair in Paris in the late 1960s and was a complete Francophile. Pretty much all our family holidays had been to France and we had never gone anywhere *near* a McDonald's. We'd stayed in rural gites in places like Normandy or Brittany or the Loire Valley where we had eaten French bread and cheese and watched a farmer's wife skin a rabbit.

Even as my mum spoke French with the locals, they had always seemed slightly *other*, slightly exotic, but now, now actually living for a week with my penfriend, I realised they weren't actually very French. I mean, not the kind of French I had always imagined the French to be, which wasn't actually French at all. It was just some kind of amalgam of Vanessa Paradis and a rabbit-skinner via an episode of *'Allo 'Allo*.

A couple of years later my sister Phoebe had a French penfriend, Marjorie. Although it never became official I would become kind of penfriends with her brother Stephane, though we never actually wrote to each other, which does seem a prerequisite of penfriendship. Anyway, they lived in a different part of France in the small town of Thonon-les-Bains, not far from Switzerland. It was the town next door to Évian-les-Bains, or Évian, of the water fame.

If anything, I liked this Stephane even more than the first. He was three years older than me and so knew all about the truly important things in life, like Jean-Claude Van Damme movies and oral sex, both of which were subjects he could talk at length on. Anyway, they lived in a nice detached suburban farmhouse on the edge of this very lovely and immaculate town. I enjoyed it more than my sister, and so returned on my own, this time to go to school in France.

School in France was brilliant, especially if you were English. I was flirted at by girls (something that *never* happened to me back in England) and made friends easily. All the teachers went out of their way to be nice to me (again, a rare occurrence back home) and then after school I would head back to the fabric shop where Stephane and Marjorie's mother, Colette, worked and speak bad French with some of the customers.

Then we'd go back and eat with their jolly rosy-faced farmer father, Jean-Paul, who drank rosé wine from a water jug as if it was, well, water. I would soon discover that they too would eat in McDonald's (in *Geneva*) but by this time I was actually craving French food, because everything they cooked at home – including snails in garlic, no less – was far more delicious than a Big Mac.

During my few weeks there I would meet more cousins and friends. I would fall in love about a hundred times and watch a lot of dubbed Jean-Claude Van Damme movies. As an adult, in the age of Facebook, I heard that Stephane and Marjorie's father Jean-Paul had died of a heart attack and that news cut me to the bone, not for my loss but for theirs, the family who had taken me in as one of their own, and given me weeks of respite during a rather miserable year (I wasn't a very popular fourteen-year-old back home, so being in France had felt like developing a happier alter ego).

France wasn't another place. It was Europe. I realised it was like England, just slightly better, and with a sexier accent. It was a little leap across a grey bit of water. They weren't strangers there. They were friends – no, *family* – in waiting. When I went home I decided I wasn't simply British, I was *European*. That instantly made me feel better, as if not only Britain was less isolated but that I was too, and as though the world and future were suddenly more open, as if the potential friend pool had been massively expanded, just from a simple switch of perspective. From that point on I would never understand why anyone would want to shrink their identity rather than broaden it.

AN EDIBLE DEBT

Bee Wilson

BEE WILSON is a food writer and historian who writes for a wide range of publications including the *London Review of Books* and the *Guardian*. She is the author of six books on food-related subjects including *First Bite: How We Learn to Eat*. She lives in Cambridge.

'English cream!' announced the waiter. I was on my first visit to Paris as a child, circa 1985, and we had ordered a dessert with crème anglaise. With infinite tact and hospitality, the waiter was suggesting that this silken sauce somehow belonged to our country and not his. This was obviously a lie, but a charming one. The pool of cold pale vanilla, which we consumed in sensuous spoonfuls, was utterly unlike the lumpen bowls of hot packet custard we knew from England.

When British grown-ups spoke of European food in the 1980s, there could be a certain tetchiness, or so I remember. They complained that everything was too garlicky or else too oily. The steak was underdone, the cheeses were smelly, the sausage was probably donkey meat and the sauces, if you weren't careful, would give you a tummyache. As for getting a decent cup of tea made from properly boiled water, hopeless! These Continentals were bohemian types who drank black coffee or red wine at strange times of day. If you asked for a piece of buttered toast, they might, laughably, think a cold crispbread would do.

What the grown-ups meant, though they could not quite bring themselves to admit it, was that European food was *delicious*. It had suave flavours and textures that we with our packet soups and post-war meat and two veg could only dream of. Europe tasted of crusty bread and sweet unsalted butter. It was seafood perfumed with wine and apricots warmed by southern sun. Even when the dishes were called the same as ours, they were not the same, because there was a subtle artistry to them that British cooks at that time either did not know or did not wish to know. A salad in France was not something plonked together from vinegary beetroot and cucumber with bottled salad cream, but a bowl of perfectly seasoned green leaves. A new potato, I discovered one lunchtime in Brittany, could be densely waxy and buttery and painstakingly 'turned', not some watery overboiled thing in its jacket.

For centuries, the upper classes in Britain had relied on French when writing menus, as if to acknowledge that it was the language of pleasure at the table. In the 1950s and 60s, Elizabeth David encouraged the British to dream anew of Continental joys in her book *French Provincial Cooking*: of 'delicate rose pink langoustines' in Normandy and the rich tarts of Alsace and Lorraine.

Yet our admiration for 'Continental' cooking was always double-edged. In 1747, the cookbook author Hannah Glasse complained that 'if Gentlemen will have French Cooks, they must pay for French Tricks'. It was long part of British self-identity to imagine that our own food had an unadorned honesty that could never be matched by the devious complexity of a Spanish paella. Elizabeth David complained, in 1960, of 'bigoted' caterers who claimed that 'English stomachs are fit only to digest roast meat, boiled vegetables and fried fish'.

Bit by bit, English stomachs got over some of their xenophobic prejudices and acclimatised to the foods of the

Continent. In just a few decades, we stopped thinking of olive oil as something sold in tiny quantities by chemists to treat earwax and started collecting whole litres of different green extra-virgins on our kitchen counters. We discovered that just because something was garlicky, that was no reason not to enjoy it. Red wine, coffee and rare steak ceased to be alien to us, whether because of cheap travel or because of the new chain restaurants that sold us fantasies of eating in Rome, even if we were really in a shopping centre in Milton Keynes. Pizza became as normal on British tables as bread. In UK supermarkets there is now often a whole chilled aisle devoted entirely to 'Italian' and, in 2016, the British consumed a third of the entire annual production of Prosecco. A product developer for British ready meals told me that one of the quickest ways to sell any new dish now is to add chorizo to it.

Our edible debt to Europe plays out in countless ways, large and small. Europeans may have joked about the awfulness of British cuisine, yet, curiously, it's partly thanks to the EU that British regional foods regained a sense of pride in recent years. British food benefited from the PDO system (protected designated origin), giving protected status to special regional foods of Europe, from Treviso radicchio to Sorrento lemons. It took Europe to remind Britons of the specialness of Herdwick lamb, Cornish clotted cream and Melton Mowbray pork pies – among more than sixty other British foods protected under European labelling.

While critics of the EU grumbled about stupid laws on 'wonky' bananas, European workers in Britain were jointing our chickens and picking our strawberries; they were swirling latte art on the top of our cappuccinos and manufacturing our ready meals. As of 2015, according to data from a briefing paper on food and Brexit by Tim Lang and Victoria Schoen, more than a quarter of those working in British food manufacturing are EU immigrants. Meanwhile, European imports are the source, as of 2015, of nearly a third of all the food eaten by value in the UK, especially the fresh produce we should be eating more of. Only 30 per cent of Britons eat 'five-a-day' of fruit and veg, but we might eat still less without easy imports of Spanish tomatoes and German pears.

Leaving the EU and its food laws would – or will? – be a task of labyrinthine complexity, from renegotiating farm subsidies to drawing up new environmental and labour laws. As Lang and Schoen have written, 'A vast array of agreements, policies and standards now underpin UK food. Labels are in EU formats. This did not just happen. It was negotiated.' European food laws left us better fed, healthier and safer than we would otherwise have been.

Yet when I think of Brexit and food, my objections are less practical than emotional. It feels sad and wrong that we should be shunning European neighbours who taught us so much about how to eat. Is this how we repay all that hospitality? All those oceans of Prosecco? The Brexit vote was – among other things – a sign of how secure the nation felt in its new European ways of eating. The British – who long ago colonised curry along with India – have now 'taken control' of European flavours. In or out of the EU, no one can steal away our mozzarella or lunchtime baguette. Pasta pesto will still be made in thousands of kitchens the length and breadth of these isles.

But something huge will be lost if we close ourselves off from this continent of pleasure. Food is not just about ingredients. It is a vast cultural exchange between peoples that plays out over dinner. We'll have no one who cares enough to translate our custard into crème anglaise.

HOW BRITISH HISTORY HAS BEEN DIFFERENT FROM EUROPEAN HISTORY

Andrew Roberts

ANDREW ROBERTS has written thirteen books, including *The Holy Fox*, *Eminent Churchillians*, *Salisbury: Victorian Titan*, *Napoleon and Wellington*, *Hitler and Churchill*, *Waterloo*, *A History of the English-Speaking Peoples Since 1900*, *Masters and Commanders*, *The Storm of War: A New History of the Second World War* and *Napoleon the Great*. He is a PhD from Caius College, Cambridge, a Fellow of the Royal Society of Literature and the Royal Historical Society, the Lehrman Institute Distinguished Fellow at the New-York Historical Society and a visiting professor at the Department of War Studies of King's College, London. His website is www.andrew-roberts.net.

On Thursday, 24 February 1848, the reign of King Louis Philippe was brought to an end as a mob looted the Tuileries Palace in Paris. 'Everything was broken up, looted and pillaged,' recorded the historian Lucas-Dubreton. 'The cellars were forced and casks broken open, with the result that the wine flowed in such quantities that some of the insurgents, already drunk, were drowned.' (Rather pleasing, that.) Right across Europe, simultaneous revolts broke out against the governments of Sicily, Naples, Holland, Milan, Venice, Berlin and Tuscany. The Austrian chancellor, Prince Metternich, was forced to flee Vienna dressed as a washerwoman. What happened in one country in Europe profoundly affected all the others.

At 11.30 a.m. on Monday, 10 April of that year, a huge political demonstration expected to number hundreds of thousands was scheduled to meet at Kennington Common in south London, which was intended to march on the Palace of Westminster and deliver a Chartist petition that had been signed by 1.2 million people. The government put the army on standby; extra guards were laid on to protect the gold in the Bank of England; the world watched closely: would Queen Victoria's government be toppled like the European ones had been?

What transpired has been described as 'a scene of drizzly pathos'; it rained and only 20,000 people turned up. The petition was delivered in four taxicabs, which the police stopped at Westminster Bridge, and everyone went home. When the petition was examined it contained obviously false names like 'Queen Victoria' and 'The Duke of Wellington', so Parliament refused to consider it. The fire that had consumed Europe – as so many times both before and afterwards – fizzled out in the very different political, historical and cultural climate of Britain.

Arthur Balfour's niece Blanche Dugdale explained British historical exceptionalism by reference to the fact that we decapitated our monarch over fourteen decades before the French did theirs, and therefore since the Glorious Revolution we already enjoyed the rights that the Europeans were agitating for throughout much of the nineteenth century – equality before the law, freedom of the press, religious toleration, limited government, a bill of rights, and so on.

Since 1789, France has had two monarchies, two empires, five republics and three invasions. The French government has been opened, shut and hurriedly moved more often than a dodgy street vendor's suitcase. In that same time period, Germany had had two republics, one monarchy, one empire, one dictatorship and two occupations, and Spain three monarchies, two occupations, one dictatorship and a civil war. Britain, meanwhile, has only had one constitutional monarchy and one empire, based all the time in Westminster. There have been no foreign armies rampaging through our islands, no civil wars or coups; evolutionary rather than revolutionary change. We've never elected a fascist to Parliament – even in the days of Oswald Mosley in the thirties – and only four communists, whereas European politics is plagued by both, and communists have entered the government in major countries such as Italy and France.

Of course much of our separate historical development can simply be put down to the inescapable fact of the twenty-two miles of the English Channel. The luck of our tectonic plate alignment as much as any seventeenth-century Whiggish constitutional genius accounts for our exceptionalism, and for the fact that the last pitched battle to have been fought on British soil took place 270 years ago at Culloden, and even that wasn't against an invader from outside.

Supporters of Brexit don't claim that Britain is better than European countries, merely that she is profoundly, politically and historically, separate and different. We wish the EU well in the way that Winston Churchill did the Iron and Steel Community in the 1950s, while he studiously kept Britain out of its coils throughout his post-war premiership. What he called 'the long continuity of our institutions' has been central to what the Queen has called the 'long history of British nationhood'. The fact that Britain has not been successfully invaded from outside these islands for 950 years – William of Orange was invited in by the Whig aristocracy in 1688 – means that, for all Tony Blair's attempt to rebrand us as a new and young country, we are in fact an old country with old ideas, customs and institutions that work, because they are generally based on compromise (as Brexit probably will be too). In a near-millennium-long history, the less than half-century blip of EU membership of 1973–2019 will be seen as the sad exception rather than the glorious rule.

Furthermore, none of the new institutions we have joined, such as the World Bank (1944), UN and IMF (1945), NATO (1949), OECD (1961) or G8 (1997) are going to be given up, and in some – such as the immensely powerful World Trade Organization (1995) – Britain will gain a newly independent voice.

Between John Cabot landing in Newfoundland in 1497 and our joining the Common Market in 1973 we had nearly five centuries of increasing global engagement, during which we made English the world language and traded or interacted in some significant way with every country in the world. The idea that we could not return to that open, confident, generous-spirited, risk-taking relationship with the rest of the planet simply because we no longer wanted 60 per cent of our laws made in Brussels is ludicrous. To deny or refuse to recognise Britain's historical exceptionalism is as absurd as to be embarrassed or ashamed of it. When we hear politicians trying to justify policies on the grounds that Britain was the only country in the EU not to conform to them, there was usually a sound historical explanation for that, a source of pride rather than embarrassment.

Europe is an important part of the British past, present and future, but not a more important part than America, Canada, New Zealand, Australia, the West Indies and many other places with which we have important ties, places that – unlike Brussels – have no desire to have ultimate power over our laws, demographics and trading relationships.

SAVING US FROM OURSELVES: EUROPE'S VALUE AND BRITAIN'S IRRATIONAL EXILE

Oliver Kamm

OLIVER KAMM is a leader writer and columnist for *The Times*. His book *Accidence Will Happen: The Non-Pedantic Guide to English* (2015) is published by Weidenfeld & Nicolson.

In a Hague courtroom one day in 2016, a quack doctor was sentenced to forty years in jail for crimes against humanity, war crimes and genocide. The career and fate of Radovan Karadžić, sometime Bosnian Serb leader, were determined by two clashing ideas of Europe. The first was his own deranged racist vision of a greater Serbia created by mass expulsion and terror; the second was its subjection to the impartial application of justice.

The genocide at Srebrenica of 8000 Bosnian Muslim men and boys in July 1995 was the greatest atrocity on European soil since the defeat of Nazism. It was aided by egregious insouciance from the international community, which failed to recognise the potentialities of evil till far too late. To his astonishment, Karadžić was eventually delivered up to justice in 2008, after years of hiding in plain sight in Serbia. The post-Milošević government in Belgrade aimed for accession to the EU; for that ever to happen, Serbia needed to demonstrably adhere to European values. It couldn't any longer harbour war criminals.

I dwell on the horrors of the Bosnian war of a quarter of a century ago because of their continuity with the worst period in the modern history of Europe. The central reason for valuing the often infuriating and sometimes dysfunctional institutions that European policymakers have built in the post-war era is pragmatic. Merely by existing, they make more difficult a reversion to the genocidal barbarism that visited this continent within living memory, and that was echoed in the massacres perpetrated by Karadžić and his criminal lieutenants.

My story will seem by comparison bathetic, but by profession I'm a pundit. I write on economics. I write often about the economic effects of Brexit on the European Union and, much more seriously (as it is the smaller party), on Britain. Like almost all economists, I believe there will be big costs for the UK in leaving the EU. Economists are fallible but we understand the mechanisms by which economies grow. By curbing the free movement of goods, services, investment and labour, Brexit will make Britain poorer than it would otherwise be. Nor is the EU just about free trade and free movement. The single market eliminates not only tariffs but the far more important non-tariff barriers to trade (like rules of origin) between its members. Exiting it makes no economic sense at all.

Economists refer to a gravity effect in trade. It means that countries trade more with economies that are close and large than they do with economies that are small and distant. British trade with Australia and New Zealand will never be remotely as important as trade with the EU. With trade in goods, the costs of shipping are an obvious reason why this should be so. But it's true with trade in services too, such as law, consultancy and accounting. Even in the digital age, clients value face-to-face contact. There is no economic sense in which Brexit can 'work'; the best that can be achieved for Britain is to limit the damage, by replicating as far as it can its current status but without the influence that EU membership confers.

All of this, however, is of secondary importance to me. I'd support European integration and Britain's full participation in it even if the economic case were weak. The European ideal matters for living standards but still more it matters for comity and human rights. The post-war institutions of Europe demonstrate the truth of John Stuart Mill's dictum that 'the economical benefits of commerce are surpassed in importance by those of its effects which are intellectual and moral'.

Those economic benefits are the gains in real incomes that trade and integration make possible, by enabling countries to specialise in the goods they produce and the services they provide. But the moral gains for post-war Europe have been vastly greater, even if intangible. Above all, the continent of Europe has not been riven by war for two generations. There is no point or plausibility in disputing the importance of the EU in eliminating historic rivalries between France and Germany. The founding statement of the institutions that eventually became the EU is the Schuman Declaration of 1950, which proposed placing French and German coal and steel production under a common higher authority. The declaration states as its first sentence: 'World peace cannot be safeguarded without the making of creative efforts proportionate to the dangers which threaten it.' Hence the initial, limited step of pooling coal and steel. Peace was the point of it; and it worked.

The pacific influence of the European ideal has been evident not only among the larger states. Conflicts with deep historical roots that once appeared intractable have been mollified, if not resolved, by European integration. Till the last years of the twentieth century, Cyprus, Ireland and the Balkans were racked by sectarian conflict. European integration has offered a better way, not only materially but by expanding intellectual and cultural horizons. The descent of the former Yugoslavia into ethnic slaughter in the 1990s wasn't a state of nature but a deliberate decision by a xenophobic regime to destroy other peoples whom they judged impure. The EU has reasserted and enabled to flourish the ethos urged by the polymaths and intellectuals of Central Europe who were dispersed by war and dictatorship in the first half of the twentieth century.

My own family has made a small contribution to the drawing together of Europe to shut out the destructiveness of its past. Martin Bell, my uncle, witnessed as a BBC war correspondent the crimes of the Milošević regime and its functionaries, and gave evidence for the prosecution in the Karadžić trial. Anthea Bell, my mother, has translated many great works of European literature into English, including the previously neglected works of Stefan Zweig. Once the most popular of European novelists, Zweig exemplified the flowering of the culture and thought of Central Europe a century ago. As his biographer George Prochnik puts it, 'the explosion of creativity in early-twentieth-century Vienna is often depicted as a kind of beautiful dream ... before some primal savagery reared up and extinguished that renaissance.' In reality, the scholars and artists of Europe were as prey to the delusions of ethnocentrism and ethnic purity as anyone, and some disgracefully gave sustenance to the myths of Nazism. To Zweig, an exponent of the ideals of Jewish universalism, it seemed literally the end of civilisation; he and his wife, Lotte, committed suicide in exile in Brazil in 1942.

Modern Europe has not abolished dispute and conflict. Any conceivable human society requires trading off competing claims to scarce resources and mediating among values that aren't compatible with each other. But the European movement has created pluralism, in which citizens of free societies are able to choose the ends of life for themselves rather than have absolutist visions of the good imposed upon them. The European ideal has been embattled lately; but it's resilient. And for me, at least, I count it a professional duty and moral obligation to oppose, thwart, impede and sabotage the efforts of those who would denigrate and undermine it.

AFTER THE WAR

Hari Kunzru

HARI KUNZRU is the author of the novels *The Impressionist, Transmission, My Revolutions, Gods Without Men* and *White Tears*. He lives in New York.

Après la guerre fini
Soldat Anglais partée,
M'selle Frongsay boko pleury,
Après la guerre fini.

Here we are, teenage Tommies on the way home, throwing up Pernod over the side of the ferry, contraband flick knives and packets of Gauloises Blondes stuffed down our pants. We're leaving Europe, coming home.

We've had enough. There's only so much paella you can stomach. What we want is beans on toast and a decent cup of tea. We want to watch our own programmes and know the words for things. Tell Mum what we got up to, then early to bed. But we did Europe, came, saw and conquered. Lads on tour. Prague, Marbella, Amsterdam. Drunk in the old town. Drunk at the station, at a sex show in the red light district. We watched a woman doing a handstand, lighting a candle in her pussy. A man in silver boots arrived and blew it out, then fucked her like it was work. Plastering, digging a hole.

In the cafe, they come and go, the descendants of Charlemagne with their little 33cl bottles of beer and their social security. We've had enough of them and their espadrilles, enough of the trattoria, the mountain hut, the little pension that's not mentioned in any of the guides. We've walked through the forum, through the dunes, past the mahogany men looking like a colony of seals in tiny red speedos. We tried not to look at their chest hair and their shower shoes and their chains and watches and phones, but what can you do? We ticked off our list. We knotted the sleeves of our sweaters so they hung casually off our backs. We looked in the windows of the designer shops, climbed the steps to the tower. We didn't mean to end up on the nudist beach. We were just looking for the place where they rent the pedalos.

We never liked the food, by the way. Or we liked it too much, the oil, the saffron, the garlic, the pungent local wines. We tasted the goat's cheese at the Saturday market. We tried different types of olive. Three days in bed, that cheese cost us. *L. monocytogenes*. High fever, soundtracked by the buzzing of the fridge, puking into mixing bowls and listening to the neighbours arguing by the pool.

We did the paseo and the Macarena. We got paranoid in the coffee shop. We bought duff pills outside the espuma party and tasted in the *caves* of the chateau. Peering through the doors of restaurants that we weren't dressed for, we settled on a place with a wall-mounted TV and set menu. After lunch we found the church with the black madonna and the Nigerians selling postcards and sunglasses. We wore long sleeves and pretended to know what the guide was saying about the Counter-Reformation. One by one we fell into the canal.

When we set out it was romantic. Boys on Vespas in holiday towns. Girls by the rides at the funfair. We drank in village bars with pinball machines. We never had enough to pay for a sandwich. A hand inside Astrid's underwear. A hand in Marco's underwear. Sylvie's hand in ours. Sleeping on our camping mats at the railway station, walking by the main road looking for a place to hitch. We passed the dirty video shop. We scored in the medieval old town, following the Arab man in the dusty brown suit through its maze of narrow streets. We took selfies at the holocaust memorial and fixed up on the steps of the former Stasi HQ. They gave us suntan lotion and retsina and an invitation to a swinger's party. We partook of all the old corruptions, read the labels by all the degenerate art. So you have to understand that we did Europe. Now we're ready for something new.

We've had enough of them coming round here, that's another thing. Apple picking, changing the bedpan, telling us about the new season's fashion trends. They can fuck off with their metric system, their Code Napoleonique. Boney in his tricorn hat, snatching the cook's leg of mutton, creeping about in the dead of night. We've had experience. *Dear Professor Wittgenstein, you are a person with no leave to enter or remain in the United Kingdom. You have not given any reason why you should be granted leave to remain. Therefore you are liable to removal. If you do not leave as required, you will be liable to enforced removal to your country of origin . . .*

Now it's Dunkirk time, small boats taking us back over, a plucky flotilla, each and every one flying the Cross of Saint George. Jerry's bombing the beaches, but we're keeping our chin up, whistling 'The Final Countdown', brave boys limping home to rationing and bitterness, just how we like it. Three channels of Saturday night variety and crying into a knotted hanky at the Proms. Beefy bouncy bloody bake-off and we'll fucking kill you if you say a word against.

So now we're all going to live together on our island. We're going to paddle our own canoe. What larks! We'll be new Elizabethans, buccaneers. Commander Ted and his crew of Swallows: John, Titty, Susan, Roger and little half-caste Bridget. Mucking about in boats all summer long. Yes we have no straight bananas, just warehouse conversions and the ghost of Cool Britannia. Our business model is based on cappuccino froth, and we know that when the banks call time the whole place will be a wasteland. What of it? Cannons to the left of us, sovereign wealth funds to the right. You can see our pimply arses, we're that exposed. But it's the will of the people, which makes it final. Henceforth we'll be pulling on our Yorkshire puds all on our ownsome, thank you very much. You'll be sorry, you Euros. You'll miss us. *M'selle Frongsay boko pleury.* Because the war's over and we're going home for tea.

BELFAST TO BERLIN AND BEYOND TO BAGHDAD AND THEN BACK AGAIN

Colonel T.T.C. Collins OBE BSc MA PSC

TIM COLLINS was born in Belfast in 1960. After university he joined the Royal Irish Rangers in West Berlin before volunteering for the Special Air Service (22 SAS) in 1988. He took part in the First Gulf War as an SAS captain. He attended the Army Command and Staff Course in UK and US in 1995. He was appointed as the operations officer of 22 SAS in 1995. Rejoining the Royal Irish in 1997 he led his company on operations in East Tyrone. Taking command of the 1st Battalion The Royal Irish Regiment in 2001, he led the battalion on operations in East Tyrone and the liberation of Iraq. He was awarded the OBE in 2003. He retired from the army in August 2004 as a colonel. Since his leaving the forces he co-founded New Century. Serving with the USMC as a civilian, Tim led his men in Iraq and Afghanistan. Tim has written a bestselling memoir *Rules of Engagement* as well as numerous TV films.

When I was first deployed in the army I had no real
feeling that I was a European. It was 1982 and I was
posted to the 2nd Battalion The Royal Irish Rangers in Berlin.
The Cold War was in a fractious mood and I found myself
in a German autumn in a vibrant but nervous city. Over the
coming months I would rub shoulders with the Berliners,
bond with the Americans, get to know the French, smile
and nod at the Russians and be glared at stared at and sometimes whispered to by the East Germans. As an Irish officer
in the British Army we felt like and were treated as just that:
The British. Different, aloof, valued and welcome – on our
side of the wall. Not European at all. And all the more welcome for that. It was a very odd place. A place of its time and
now is long passed.

I had of course visited Europe as a scout on several occa-
sions. I had also led a gaggle of my fellow students to Brussels
and Strasbourg on a visit to European Union Institutions in
my capacity as secretary to the Economics Society at Queen's
University Belfast, but now here I was living and working in a
European city – well, sort of, as part of the army of occupation.

One might imagine that the local Berliners would be surly
and resentful. They were quite the opposite. They marvelled

and enjoyed the spectacle of our not infrequent parades or band concerts – we, the Irish, had both a band made up of professional musicians and a separate bugle pipe and drum band manned by soldiers. The other British regiments had their own version on the theme.

Life in Berlin then was closely scripted to events and sporting fixtures, including a rotation to guard the single prisoner in Spandau Prison – former Deputy Führer Rudolph Hess. We would relieve the Russians and would hand over to the French who would pass the guard to the Americans who would be relieved by the Russians. It was a pretty onerous and boring task for the men – ours would have to clean the place up after the Russians, unblock the toilets and clear the cabbage strewn around the cookhouse while the officers might be able to catch a glimpse of the old boy himself when he was exercising in the yard. I say exercising – he shuffled along on a Zimmer-frame dressed in après-ski boots and a duvet jacket the only time I met him, on 30 January 1983 – the fiftieth anniversary of the Nazis coming to power. I recall him as a bowed old man with malevolent blue eyes staring out from under massive bushy eyebrows. We were not allowed to speak to him nor he us. He derived what little fun he had by following me around the orchard at the back of the prison staring intently. As I walked I would occasionally glance around to find him staring with a grimace. I guess it was his thing (he didn't get out much you see).

We thought ourselves pretty superior as a military then. The Americans were just transitioning as an all-professional army from conscription; the French and Russians were reluctant conscripts. Our troops in contrast were all volunteers, mine overwhelmingly Irish, delighted to be in work; thrilled to be out of Ireland, in what was to us exotic Berlin. Perhaps it was that, perhaps not, but the mood of the city folk seemed to closely follow the activity of our troops. Planned and advertised training was closely followed – and sometimes applauded by the Germans. Surprise deployments, often at night – Operation Rocking Horse serial – would always be tragically attended by several Berliners throwing themselves out of apartment blocks or onto railway lines, fearing that the manoeuvres were for real and resolving never to live under the Soviets again.

Frequently we would board trains to pass through the corridor into West Germany to take part in military exercises, often with allies – Belgians and Germans mostly. Once more conscripts, all absolutely disinterested, the Belgians sparsely equipped, the Germans in their superb Marder Panzergrenadier fighting vehicle and Leopard tanks, but lolling about smoking and carping to us in English with semi-American accents.

One of the highlights was going in the opposite direction and visiting the East. It was a mixture of buildings – some smashed by the bombing of the war thirty-seven years before, mostly churches and cathedrals – and hideous tiled Soviet apartment blocks, with here and there restored buildings from Prussia's heyday. We would be required to wear uniform when going East, smart jackets, cross belts and shined up brogues by day. Mess kit at night with scarlet jackets and spurred boots. It was very cheap with one pound worth 16 East Marks, four times what a West Mark was worth. But there was nothing really to buy except food and beer. The fare was cheap and basic. In the smarter restaurants you could eat venison and drink Romanian wine by finding out beforehand which ones had other than sausage, while being stared at by long tables of East German workers being treated, perhaps for meeting production targets, feasting on the inevitable sausage and cabbage and beer. In the street or the pubs it was poor quality German sausages with mustard off thin brown cardboard and wooden forks. The cars, Trabants or 'Trabis', were also made of cardboard and wood.

The Volkspolizei – 'VoPo' – watched us with menace. The people's army conscripts would whack you with the antenna of a tank if you got too close during one of their parades, but the grey East Berliners in the pubs would try to carry out a whispered conversation, marvelling at your clothes and cadging cigarettes as they glanced around the room watching out for plain clothes Stasi. Jeremy Corbyn would have loved the place. Everyone was equally fucked.

Now it is all times past. But this experience shaped my expectation of European soldiers and European militaries for the future. Looking back over my career I served many times in multinational operations in Cyprus, Bosnia, Kosovo, Iraq and Afghanistan. My expectation was largely met. While the European armies have professionalised over the years, little had changed. In the central headquarters of Sarajevo, Baghdad Green Zone or Kabul Airport the multinational camps would be packed to capacity and feature coffee bars, beer bars and national shops. For the most part, only the British and Americans would routinely leave the camps on operations, and out in the wilds there were only the usual suspects: the UK, Yanks and, in Afghanistan, the Canadians and up in the hills the Australians. In fairness in Afghanistan, the Czechs and Poles would deploy pretty aggressive special forces. The Danes did get out and around in Helmand until political pressure to avoid casualties curbed their activities. The New Zealand and Norwegian special forces pretty much matched anything the SAS did, but the rest stayed firmly in camp smoking and carping.

Berlin is unrecognisable now. To say it is multicultural is an understatement, and it is difficult to find a Berliner at all. Everyone is from somewhere else in the world it seems. The bases in the West that once hosted the British Army are now mostly refugee centres, and the town centres of German cities are very diverse. Visiting Munich during a beer festival last spring one could not but feel discomfort at the gangs of young Arabs and Somalis huddled in the city squares glaring disapprovingly at the Germans drinking and smoking, spitting on the ground aggressively if you strayed too close. It is hard to imagine that long gone world of Cold War Europe. In hindsight it does not seem such a bad place. However now, as in 1982, I still don't feel very European. We are very different. I don't think they will notice when we are gone. I doubt we'll be missed.

FOUND IN TRANSLATION

Jessie Burton

I puked up a snail the first time I went to France. This isn't a metaphor, to convey to you by story how I voted Leave, for I did not. We were ten years old, a mixed bunch; state primary school kids, many of whom had never ventured past the white cliffs. Throughout the build-up to this exotic trip, and on the water over, mine and my classmates' imaginations riveted on the fact the French ate snails. All of the French-type people did. Probably every day.

I was already obsessed with foreign language; I liked the magic spell of weird words, uttering them, having them understood, thus being transported onwards into an exciting situation. *Où est la pâtisserie?* was an incantation that led to chocolate eclairs. These were good words, unlike the words that were to come, and there was an orderliness to vocabulary tests that salved me. But my early love of the foreign coalesced primarily into this garlic snail, which it turned out I could not abide. It was not a happy-looking prospect, but I was going to eat it, if it was the last thing I did. The next morning, the regurgitated mollusc was streaked upon my pillow.

Three years after the snail, I went on a proper French exchange, and also hated every minute. I was homesick, my host family had a thing for taxidermied stoats, stark overhead lighting and hair-spraying their fringes, and there weren't many nice eclairs to be had. It was in the Champagne region, so they kept plying me with the stuff and nicknamed me *La Rouge*. (If only I'd done the exchange ten years later: I'd have made far more of this blessing of the land, and happily owned the moniker.) When my French counterpart came to stay with me in London, she became obsessed with Hovis sliced bread. It was, for her, literally the best thing since. She asked for toast, constantly. My mother, whose French was workable with occasional surrealist flourishes, told the girl not that she was full, but that she was a pregnant pig. Never again have I heard a young person laugh, so much, in a land that was strange to them. But how clearly I understood her joy.

The snail, the taxidermied stoats, the fact you might tell someone you were a pregnant pig, did not put me off. None of it was comfortable, but I was born better to mimic others than to inhabit myself, so I took my French GCSE early and studied Spanish for my degree, living in Andalusia and working as an English assistant in a school. The children (one of whom was a trainee bullfighter) would roll their eyes at me, and say, *maestra*, your language is crazy. Our inconsistent rules of pronunciation had them flummoxed. *Though through the rough, thorough will I plough!* Those children taught me, in ways that I had never questioned, how English, like the land it sprang from, squat cottage, slender high-rise, loved both exception and hybridity. English wanted it all.

So when the Brexit result came through the rough, perhaps I should not have been as surprised as I was. It was the same week as the publication of my second novel. And while only one of these events, alas, had a seismic international impact,

I was to go round the UK flogging my book as my country flogged itself. At the launch party, in a room overlooking the Mall, from whose balconies we could see Buckingham Palace and hear the bells of Big Ben, the metropolitan elite looked shocked and saddened. These bookish people, traders in ideas, soft on a croissant and a glass of good wine! They dreamed of sunshine and cypresses. They never saw it coming. I had to rewrite my speech and talk about what happened. The good words were gone. I was angry about how inflammatory words could lead a man to murder a woman while yelling *Britain First*, of how deceitful words on the side of a campaign bus could lie outright to the public and get away with it. Words, twisted in the mouths of men, had led to darker depths we hadn't seen for years.

The week before, I'd sat with my French editor, who confidently told me that of course we would remain, we would stay, we wouldn't ever do such a thing! We could surely see the bigger picture, could taste history's dangers on our collective tongue. But we did do such a thing. *We* being a moot word, of course, another abstraction. Nothing since the abdication of Edward VIII, exactly seventy years before, had Britain been so exposed to her longstanding, painful divisions riveting through her island and, in many cases, the families she bore. 'The British people' was a nice concept, but it was exactly that, vapour turned to vitriolic newsprint, an alchemic act that transformed the words on that bloody bus into the 'will of the people', a battering ram for politicians to claim an unimpeachable mandate to kick the EU in the balls and run off, cackling.

We really hated politicians that summer, I remember. Not

all of them, but a lot of them. And do you remember the house of cards spilling, so many prime ministers in one month? What did we have, one, two, six, ten? I cannot recall. Their faces interchanged, floppy-haired, pink-faced, bug-eyed and fakely confident as they realised in shock how their performances had paid off, before unzipping their disguises like *Scooby-Doo* villains and running off to their lives, resigning, changing jobs, again and again, again, again. It was an execrable show of entitlement, complacency, buck-passing and self-interest, and the public paid for it. The inner rhythms of British life had gone completely haywire. Nothing prepared us for it, and nothing had been prepared after it. If Brexit was a novel, my editor would have told me to revise its lack of nuance in pace and villainy.

I won't dwell on villains. I won't even dwell on the EU. Because truth be told, when I think about Europe, I do not think about the 'EU'. *Europe*, in common with words such as *Churchill*, *getting-your-country-back*, *Britain* – and let's face it, *Hovis* – is a part of our language not easily rooted in a daily reality. Instead of fact, emotion rises to the surface, just as it did for the French journalist who sat with me in Paris on the day Article 50 was triggered, and asked forlornly, in English, 'Why don't you like us?' The importance of emotion in *débâcles* such as these should never be underestimated.

I think impressionistically, magically, about snails and *siestas* and *cartes postales*, hot streets, beaches and canals. Queues for museums. Brigitte Bardot. I think as magically about this as a Leaver might have thought about bunting and coffers full of shillings for the NHS. I too am part of England, English, British; and I too want it all. I love Hovis and Cheddar, and

Europe is my baguette, my mozzarella. Europe is my bistro of brass and mirrors, where the maître d' makes sure I have my favourite table. England is stone and moss and literature, battlements, a scone. Europe is heat and art and marble. Both are age and blood, dreamscapes we straddled for decades. Europe to me was a light; it wasn't a regulation on the candescence of my bulbs. I understood that to have it all, to have it there if I wanted it, there was a compromise. Wasn't it a way, in the wake of a century that changed everything, forever, that we could live closer to an ideal? Wasn't it an agreement? Yes, and it was trade. And if *that's* idealist, if *that's* being soft on a croissant, then fine. Because what the hell is left for us in this day and age?

It might all be fine. Maybe we'll all get crowns in the post from the extra millions we've saved and, self-crowned, heavy-headed, take charge of our destiny. Someone, somewhere, will be paying the price, though, and my guess is it isn't the people who got this ball rolling. So we must hold on to the chaos of pregnant pigs for the generations to come, and guard for them the hedonistic, diplomatic offerings of sliced toast. We must make our ten-year-olds eat those snails, and bring them out of their shells. We must think about the velvet ribbons we have severed. We must think about the water. Above all, what I feel is this: we must use good words.

A LOSS FOR WORDS

Kate Eberlen

KATE EBERLEN grew up in a small town near London and spent her childhood longing to escape to the big city. She spent a year in Rome as an au pair before studying Classics at Oxford University. Kate has lived in London, New York and Madrid, working in many different fields, including publishing and teaching English as a Foreign Language. She now divides her time between England and Italy. Kate is the author of *Miss You*, which was selected for the Richard and Judy Summer Bookclub 2017, and is an international best-seller published in thirty languages.

Playing word games on long car journeys feels like a very British thing to do, but perhaps every culture has its own version of this pastime. In our family, when we've exhausted I Spy but still have many miles to travel, we sometimes dream up questions such as 'If you could meet one famous person from the whole of history, who would it be?' More thought than you might expect is involved in responding. While your instant reaction might be Nelson Mandela, when you start imagining what you would actually learn from such an encounter, you might find yourself veering in the direction of Jane Austen or Julius Caesar instead.

An ostensibly simple question such as 'If you had to eat only one meal every day for the rest of your life, what would it be?' also demands precision and clarification of the rules. If, for example, I say 'fruit' for dessert, would it then be legitimate for me to eat a different fruit each day, or do I have to specify a seasonal fruit salad to achieve that variety?

And sometimes the issue is yet more complex. Five years ago, when we were travelling to Palermo airport after a particularly good holiday in Sicily, my son, then sixteen, asked: 'If you could either live the rest of your life in the UK and never leave, or live abroad and travel as much as you wanted, but never be allowed to return to the UK, which would you choose?'

We had just spent two weeks gazing at panoramic views, visiting fascinating ruins, bathing in warm, crystalline seas, shopping in bustling markets, eating leisurely al fresco lunches, tasting fabulous ice cream, watching spectacular sunsets, so the answer appeared to be a no-brainer.

And yet I hesitated, pondered, and eventually replied: 'I think I'd have to stay in the UK.'

'But WHY?'

The dismay on my son's face was so palpable, I felt I'd lost any claim I'd ever had to being a cool mother and would now forever be cast as tragic.

So, I was required to justify my reasons.

I would miss my family and friends. ('But they could travel.')

I would miss London – the art, the theatre, the ballet. ('But you'd have a choice of Paris, Berlin, Venice, Rio, St Petersburg, New York!')

I want to live in an open, tolerant, liberal democracy. ('But so are lots of countries! Italy, for example. You love it here!')

Ultimately, I decided, it was about language. It's not that I don't like learning new languages – I love the challenge – but I've always considered myself lucky to have been born a native speaker of English. It has many more words than others and allows such scope for nuance, irony and humour. As a writer and English language teacher, I am, quite literally, sustained by it. To be myself, I told my son, I needed to be able to express myself fully and freely. And, since the rules of the game demanded I choose, and since I identified culturally and linguistically as a UK citizen, I would ultimately have to opt to remain.

I then breathed a sigh of relief, thankful that this was never going to be a decision I would actually have to make.

Four years later, in the week running up to the EU referendum, I found myself back in Italy, researching a novel. I had lived in Rome in my gap year, and sometimes returning to a place where you've had a good time can be a disappointment, but the city was better than I remembered, or perhaps I was more able to appreciate it. I loved wandering along cobbled streets, turning a corner and finding myself looking at the Coliseum. I spent hours in Santa Maria Antiqua in the Forum studying the continuum of religious observation through ancient, medieval and modern times, our shared European culture emerging from the walls of one tiny church.

The streets were teeming with people from all over the world: tourists in the Piazza Navona and rich international shoppers in the Via dei Condotti, just as there had been when I'd lived there years before – but now I was struck by the fact most of the waiters were not native Italians, most of the kitchen staff seemed to come from Asia, the selfie-stick sellers from Africa. It felt as if Rome had returned to its global origins – colourful and hectic, but nowadays generally tolerant. Italians are welcoming, on the whole believing that those in need deserve kindness, that drowning people should be rescued from the sea. On my last evening, I rang my husband from the top of the Vittorio Emanuele monument at sunset and said that I thought it would be interesting to live in Rome for a while.

'If we still can, after tomorrow!' he replied gloomily.

Gazing over the eternal, rose-gold city that is so central to our European heritage, I dismissed his fears.

For me, the first indication that things were taking an unexpected turn was the extraordinary weather across southern England the next day. Unusually forceful thunderstorms delayed my flight and flash flooding closed transport links. Arriving at Gatwick in light summer clothes and sandals, I was drenched in the run from shuttle bus to car. The roads were choked; progress painfully slow; ominous clouds threatened worse to come. My car broke down in the middle lane of the M3 in rush hour. When I eventually arrived home, I was too exhausted from my journey to stay up for the result of the referendum.

The following morning, I opened my eyes, felt a slight thud of disappointment at finding myself no longer in Rome. When my husband said, 'We're leaving,' I felt as if I'd woken up in a country I didn't recognise, with a language I no longer understood.

'Brexit' – a neologism I loathe as much for its lazy inaccuracy (surely UKexit, if anything?) as for its implications – has redefined some of our most important words.

'Experts' are no longer to be trusted.

A politician on the *Today* programme refers, unchallenged, to 52 per cent as 'the overwhelming majority of the population'.

'Best possible deal' means, certainly in the short term, significantly worse economic conditions.

It is not 'patriotic' to challenge a cabinet minister.

'Getting on with the job' means putting everything on standstill for eight weeks for an unnecessary general election, destabilising the country, then pursuing the same narrow agenda despite failure to achieve a mandate.

The phrase 'democratic decision' is routinely deployed against the concerns of the majority of young people, including those who were not even old enough to vote, but whose lives will be most affected.

In a divided nation, advice to 'unite' sounds more like 'Shut up, or else . . . !'

Is it a sense of humour failure to object to the term 'Remoaner'? It's a word that comes from our exuberant tradition of tabloid puns. Even if you disagree with the politics, you admire the verbal dexterity. But is it really clever or amusing to belittle the passionately held views of so many people? And who is actually laughing at the crudely undiplomatic throwaway lines of our Foreign Secretary? Nobody in Europe, for sure. And yet, back in Rome again recently, I sensed less offended hostility than bewildered pity. Trying to explain what was happening in our country, I found myself, for the first time in my life, at a loss for words.

Would you prefer to live in the UK and never leave, or travel abroad but never come back, is still a choice I don't have to make, but in a nation that has replaced discussion with bullying, nuance with slogans, consensus with triumphalism, it is almost beginning to feel as if I do. If my son, who now lives in France – while he still can – were to ask me the question again, I'm no longer sure what my answer would be.

IN THE UNION OF FACELESSNESS

Will Self

WILL SELF is a writer and broadcaster, he lives in London.

I remember being in Ukraine, in the springtime. It was cold and I hadn't brought the right clothing. I was doing a story on Chernobyl to mark the twenty-fifth anniversary since the reactor meltdown. Around the abandoned nuclear power station lay a flat and wooded lake land full of mutant mushrooms and tremulous deer. Together with the photographer – a daredevil Russian woman – I ascended the twenty-two storeys of a derelict tower block in the abandoned city of Pripyat. At the top, we stood beneath a massive and rusting hammer and sickle bolted to a wonky structure of steel girders. In every direction the forest marched away, spiky firs and skinny, silvery birches – the lakes shone dully between their trunks. Later, I interviewed a babushka who lived in a remote shack on the banks of a turbid river. Yes, she conceded, things had been pretty bad in the aftermath of the catastrophe – and yes, she did think there'd probably been a lot more illnesses and fatalities as a result of the radioactive leak than the authorities had ever admitted to. Talking to her, while her adult son chopped wood in the small yard, I shivered – I was physically chilled, but I also felt the atmosphere was uncanny: the babushka looked old enough to have been a child during the Second World War, when the Red Army and the Wehrmacht crossed and recrossed these trackless wastes, harrowing the benighted people again and again. I'd little doubt that Chernobyl was one of the rather less appalling visitations in this longsuffering woman's long life.

I thought of Elem Klimov's masterful film *Come and See* (1985), which portrays the Nazi invasion of this region through the eyes of a child, who witnesses the soldiers descending into a carnivalesque whirl of evil deeds, which culminates in drunkenly demonic abandon, as they herd peasants into a church and set fire to it. I thought of the hotel room in Kiev where I'd spent the previous night – its window looked out over the site of Babi Yar, the ravine where the Einsatzgruppen and their Ukrainian collaborators had, in September 1941, murdered 30,000 Jews in two days. But most of all I thought how glad I was my great-grandfather had decided to get the fuck out of here in the 1890s. Like many descendants of the exilic Jews of Central Europe, I know next to nothing about my forebears – of this line all we have is his prayer book (he was a devout man – a cantor in the synagogue), with this inscription in the flyleaf: 'Vilna – Odessa – Havana – New York', and the dates for each leg of the family's journey. So it goes – the great and global swirling of the human race over the past two millennia. My family tree seems to me no rooted thing, dug into a single sod, but a fungal rhizome threading through Europe's soil: we come and we go, and we loop back once more. Even my family name – drawn from my paternal thread – speaks of this transitory affiliation, 'Self' being not a proper form of the common English noun, but a contraction of 'sea wolf', the name given by the Anglo-Saxons to their Norse invaders. An Aryan Semite – that's me.

And when I was a little bit older than the boy in Klimov's film, I smoked Gauloise Disque Bleu, drank cappuccino, and wandered around my north London suburb with one Penguin Classic or another prominently displayed in my jacket pocket. I read by imprint rather than author – so I absorbed the European canon indiscriminately; and studying philosophy rather than English literature at university sent me further in this pan-European direction. I never had any problem with the idea of a European state. No, really. We try, at the micro-level, to control our lives; and, at the macro one, we often comfort ourselves with idea that together we might – just might – be strong. But strong in which way? I can't think of any state in history that didn't come into existence because of either the need to repel an external invader, or suppress an internal rebellion; it's in states' nature, given their fundamental *raison d'être* is – as Thomas Hobbes averred – to enact a monopoly on the profession of violence. I remember long and drunken nights during the Balkan Wars of the early 1990s – I felt then as I do now: Europe stood on the brink, an inchoate entity, half-summoned into being to lay to rest the demons of our own bellicosity; now there was an opportunity for the Union to take a more cohesive form – after all, its manifest destiny was clearly incommensurate with concentration camps being erected near to our holiday destinations.

But no: it was left to American firepower to secure the borders of these new-old fissiparous statelets – just as it was left to the European Union to confirm its warped Atlanticism by adventitiously absorbing most of Russia's former Eastern Bloc 'allies' within a few short years of the Berlin Wall coming down. In 2015 I walked the route the Wall once zigzagged through the city. It was another opportunity to generate copy, of course: that's what we writers do. In Ukraine I'd felt cold – in Berlin I had one, and was accompanied by my German translator, Gregor Hens, rather than a Russian photographer. The deep fissuring of Germany after 1945 is still evident in Berlin's built environment – but stronger still is the impression that this is, indeed, the capital of a major European nation which went collectively insane in the 1930s, and after attempting to subjugate the entire continent, ended up being razed to the ground by the Red Army. There are a few stretches of the Wall left standing for touristic purposes – and at the East Side Gallery, a section running along the river covered with graffiti, there are small stalls set up where they sell fragments of this once terrifying political boundary. A stallholder told me that the city council holds an auction every year at which they bid for remaining chunks to be still further reduced into souvenirs.

Politicians who bloviate on matters European from the green benches of the House of Commons, or the greener fields of the English shires, seem to me strange creatures: unable any more to see the pasts they are doomed to recreate, so wreathed are they in the diaphanous veils of their own resurgent nationalism. And English nationalism has always been a bizarre and atemporal phenomenon – a nostalgia-tinged hankering not for a place that might be reached, but a time which never existed: a Merrie Englande, wherein knights were bold, ladies ladylike and society cheerfully organic; while in distant lands – employing our sometime Foreign Secretary, Boris Johnson's choice epithet – piccaninnies with watermelon smiles cheerfully bore the imperial yoke. Such fantasies were embodied in the bastard architectural style fathered by William Morris and the Arts and Crafts movement, and dubbed 'Tudorbethan'. It's no coincidence, I think, that I grew up in a Tudorbethan suburb – far from Vilna (which is in present day Byelorussia) – and given my mongrel blood, as I escaped its claustrophobic confines, I became more and more aware of the fundamental deception underlying English nationalism. Yet I too feel a nostalgia for a time that never existed – namely an era when Europe was happily united, at least in my own mind.

QUITTING EUROPE

Adam Dant

ADAM DANT is an internationally renowned artist whose work can be found in the collections of Tate Britain, Musee D'Art Contemporain, Lyon, Deutsche Bank and UK Parliament. His recent commissions have seen him working as the official artist of 'The Queen's Jubilee Thames Pageant' on behalf of the Port of London authority, as 'The Official 2015 General Election Artist' for The Speaker's Advisory Committee on Works of Art and in 2016 as Artist in Residence for Christie's on their 250th anniversary. Adam quit smoking fifteen years ago.

Sweet Afton / Ireland

I didn't know any artists when I was a teenager. My girlfriend kept telling me interesting stories about a friend of her family who was an artist. His name was Ernie. I think he was a Dubliner who lived somewhere in Yorkshire. Ernie became a hero and a role model to us, even though we only had one of his drawings to study. It was a charcoal portrait of my girlfriend's mother. When Ernie and his wife, who was a nurse, visited us in Cambridge I was quite nervous. At the pub I offered Ernie a cigarette, he told me that if I wanted to be a Great Artist then I should smoke Sweet Aftons, they were from Dundalk he told me, 'Flow gently, sweet Afton, among thy green braes, / Flow gently, I'll sing thee a song in thy praise'. I bought a pack from Colin Lunn, the tobacconist on King's Parade. Lovely cigarettes in a beautiful primrose yellow box. But really, way too dear for art students who could get ten Dunhills from the machine at The Live and Let Live for 50 pence.

Gauloises / France

After school had finished my girlfriend and I ran away to Paris. I think we were about sixteen or seventeen. We had a hundred quid to last us two weeks, she had an emergency hundred hidden in her shoe but only told me about it when we were on the ferry home.

We bought cigarettes from Gare Saint-Lazare, the soft blue packet had 'a picture of Asterix's hat on it'. We smoked them in our room at the Hotel des Fleurs and watched from the window the snaking queue of Arab men outside a brothel.

I smoked Gauloises for a few weeks after returning home until I lit one at my grandma's house. My father ran to open the window shouting 'Flaming Nora! What kind of bohemian, foreign compost is that?'

Gitanes / France

When my extremely chic *parigot* neighbours inevitably moved back to Paris they invited me to make an exhibition in an ex-fortune teller's booth they'd discovered for rent up the Passage des Panoramas. They were now both in proper employment. He had found a position at Chanel and had purchased an expensive Barrow and Hepburn briefcase which he carried with him everywhere.

A couple of years later, while sharing Japanese lunch in a very unfashionable businessman's restaurant, I asked him what he kept in the briefcase, which was beside his seat half-slid under the pink tablecloth. He picked it up, snapped the clasps and opened the lid to reveal that the briefcase was empty except for a carton of 200 Gitaines.

'I couldn't think of anything better to put in it,' he told me.

Ducados / Spain

I thought I'd surprise a girl I really wanted to marry by asking her to come with me to Barcelona as soon as she had landed in London from the States.

Princess Diana had just been killed the day before. The Spanish tobacconist kept going on and on about 'Le Dee-Dee . . . Le Dee-Dee' he dabbed his eye, Baptiste-style, with a pretend handkerchief. That was when my wife-to-be spotted the moulded hollow plastic chicken alarm clock in the dusty glass cabinet behind him, 'I want that chicken . . . I have to have it' and once the tobacconist had showed us what the chicken did I remember she said 'Sold!' It was the first time I'd heard anyone who wasn't an auctioneer say that.

The chicken alarm clock *cockadoodledooed* in the morning and when one popped down its red plastic comb said '*Buenos dias*'. There was a slot in its crooked wing to hold a disposable lighter in readiness for one's first cigarette of the day. We were smoking Ducados. The church bells had already woken us.

SG Ventil / Portugal

A lot of British artists had been flown out to Portugal by the British Council for a big exhibition opening at Belém. After the reception, drifting across the city from one event to another, I was fortunate to be befriended by the young Lisboa Art Gentry. At a local bar, which appeared to consist of nothing more than a makeshift counter and a shelf of bottles and glasses, we smoked the local SG cigarettes, spoke about art and listened to a woman with a guitar wailing in the corner.

One of the Portuguese artists told me that during the Salazar era, possession of a cigarette lighter had been a criminal offence. She then went on to tell me how she felt that I possessed a deep sadness inside me. I told her she was mistaken and that it must be the smoke and the music.

MS / Italy

One of the most desperate, hilarious and confounding moments in my life as a smoker came when I realised that 'MS' on Italian cigarettes did not stand, as locals told me, for '*Merde Secco*' but for '*Monopoli di Stato*', that the workers at the state tobacco warehouses had gone on strike and that the lovely couple who owned the tabbachi at the end of my street were rapidly running out of fags. They apologised sincerely and suggested I walk a bit further into Parioli to their friend's shop. Their friend quickly ran out of stock and after I found myself walking for over an hour in the morning to a gas station near the ring road, having the mafia demand 100,000 lira for a pack of Albanian counterfeit Marlboro Lights and returning to my print workshop to find my studio mate attempting to make roll ups from ancient, dried-up pipe tobacco, I decided to quit.

But not before sending postcards to as many friends and family members as possible inviting them to spend a couple of days in Rome, on the condition that their journey took them via the duty-free shop.

Prince / Denmark

In the midst of the painful and prolonged Italian tobacco

strike when all of the shelves of all of the tabbachi had been completely divested of stock and the price of a black market packet of Marlboro Lights matched my monthly stipend, I suddenly came up with a brilliant idea. My uncle was a sailor, I remembered when I was a small child him telling me that as well as sailing the Baltic that he often stopped at ports on the Mediterranean and the Adriatic. I telephoned my aunt who told me that my Uncle Bob was just leaving Copenhagen for Italy. Very soon I was in Anzio in the galley of Bob's ship with a couple of fellow nicotine-starved artists and George, a teenage archeologist whose wealthy parents had sent him to dig in Italy during his gap year. We spent the day drinking wine and brandy, listening to my uncle's stories and smoking Danish Prince cigarettes. We headed back to Rome with copious cartons. When George's Italian odyssey ended and his well-heeled parents came to collect him he handed me a small parcel. 'This is for you,' he said. 'Don't tell my parents I smoke.' I unwrapped the package to find a fag-ash-lined Colosseum ashtray and a Trevi Fountain lighter.

Belinda / Holland

On an art school trip to Amsterdam I wanted to understand how the actual layout of the city worked and why in reality it felt nothing like how it looked on the map to me.

I had a good wander around and in the process found some excellent bars.

When all the other students were discussing what to do that evening I told them that I'd discovered a fantastic Spanish place which had a huge picture of a goat on the wall.

After an hour of enjoying Amsterdam's picturesque canals my patient but slightly agitated and thirsty colleagues were relieved to hear my confident (in not knowing where the hell we were going) cry of 'The goat, the goat!' The huge picture of the goat was there for all to see through a window, on the other side of the canal. The Spanish hosts were pleased to see me again, especially with such a big group of patrons for their quiet bar.

After a tapas dinner I offered all the smokers in our number a Belinda. None of the other students had seen this brand before; they were graphic designers and were in awe of the girl on the packet. We assumed this was the eponymous Belinda. Aryan, gamine, in a white roll-neck she emerged from an orange oval holding the cigarette which shared her name with an affected crook of the wrist.

PARIS, *JE T'AIME* . . . BUT IT TOOK A WHILE

Sanjeev Bhaskar

SANJEEV BHASKAR is a writer and actor. He is probably best known for his TV series *Goodness Gracious Me*, *The Kumars at Number 42*, *The Indian Doctor* (all BBC) and the crime drama series *Unforgotten* (ITV). His West End stage work includes *Art* (Whitehall Theatre) and *Spamalot* (Palace Theatre). His first book *India with Sanjeev Bhaskar* was a *Sunday Times* bestseller based on a documentary series of the same name. He has also had a number 1 in the pop charts with 'Spirit in the Sky' (with Gareth Gates for Comic Relief) in 2003. Sanjeev is also the current chancellor of Sussex University.

The view from the Eiffel Tower. Strolling along the Champs-Élysées. Walking hand in hand along the Seine. Passion straining at the leash to the backdrop of a slate grey sky, all accompanied by the melancholy endeavours of an accordion. A city for lovers to fall in love, to fall apart and then to fall in love all over again. Ahh Paris.

It was with this catalogue culled from popular culture that I travelled to the city deemed so beautiful that it escaped even Adolf's ritual mutilation. I was twenty, had saved up from Saturday jobs to spend five days with my first love, Holly, who was living in Paris for the sandwich year of our degree.

As the train asthmatically pulled into Gare du Nord, my celluloid imagination was already presenting me with options of greetings – a cool Belmondo-style saunter as Holly ran towards me; me running towards her, arms akimbo Jerry Lewis style; both of us standing, staring at each other, the crowds and Gauloises smoke cleared from the monochrome frame. These images evaporated with every shove from the other passengers as we alighted and cascaded along the platform.

Holly was waiting on the other side of the melee, behind the barrier. I hugged her, briefly, my rucksack sliding down my back and the straps pulling my arms down, so I ended up standing to military attention.

'These are Métro passes and here's a map of Paris, I couldn't get time off work so I'll meet you afterwards, I've marked it on the map for you.' She paused. 'It's good to see you.'

With that she turned and became just another dab in the impressionistic painting that was the morning rush hour.

I was in a city for the first time, in a country for the first time, where I didn't speak the language and had eight hours to kill. Still, at the other end of today's adventure, I would be with Holly.

I stumbled around for hours, managing not to find a single famous landmark, pausing only to finish off the remnants of my packed lunch. I finally found a train station and stared at the Métro map like it was a Picasso, trying to make sense of it. I spotted the suburban station of Fontenay-aux-Roses, about forty-five minutes from central Paris and my love nest for the next five days, and promptly took the wrong train. A couple of hours later, I heroically knocked on the door of Holly's single room.

Holly looked beautiful. Before I could tell her that, the room was invaded by a gaggle of smart young French folk, all sharing the hostel amenities. They were friendly, welcoming and spoke next to no English, though they had the ability, I later discovered, to sing along with English pop songs with unnerving clarity.

At some point during the communal Camembert and baguette, Holly informed me that she would be working all week and that I could amuse myself during the day and she would meet me in the evenings. How come she hadn't taken any time off? She knew I was coming. Couldn't she throw a sickie? No, this was frowned upon. And as she started work at 8.30, an early night would be best.

So at an ungodly hour on my second day in the *ville de l'amour* I found myself, once again, staring at the Métro map, this time looking like it was the circuit diagram of the Apollo V. I'd be meeting Holly later for an intimate dinner out. Just another eight hours to kill.

Paris was beautiful – manicured gardens, Gothic, baroque, belle époque and art deco architecture, and considered breathing space around the monuments. However, I was on a budget and wondering which landmarks I should visit alone or wait to share with Holly. Conclusion: see nothing. It was, however, an opportunity to test out my phrase book. I mastered three responses with what I regard as a good ear for accents. *Je ne suis pas d'ici*, *Pardon. Je ne parle pas Français* and *Parlez-vous Anglais?*

The limitations of my phrasebook became apparent very quickly. Unless the response was one of the three prescribed answers you were in trouble.

Quels sont les spéciaux aujourd'hui
(*What are the specials today?*)
Aujourd'hui nous avons . . .
(*Today we have . . .*)
Poulet au vin blanc
(*Chicken in white wine*)
Rouget
(*Red mullet*)
Ragoût de saucisse de Toulouse
(*Toulouse sausage stew*)

I retreated to a McDonald's and Le McChicken Sandwich. Not in my phrasebook but about the only foodstuff I could recognise.

I met Holly around 6 p.m. I also met the large group of her friends that were now accompanying us on our intimate dinner. One man, Claude, spoke a little English. He seemed reserved but affable nonetheless.

In the restaurant I sat opposite Claude. To my right, on the next table, was a group of Americans from Boston. I started chatting to them, grateful for some fluid conversation. At one highpoint of surreality, I became the 'translator' between the American lady and Claude, despite both of them speaking in English:

Boston lady: Where does he come from in France?
Me: Where do you come from in France?
Claude: I come from ze Sud de France.
Me: He comes from the South of France.
Boston lady: How long has he lived in Paris?
Me: How long have you lived in Paris?
Claude: Two yers and sree mounths.
Me: Two years and three months.

The food arrived. It was, well, raw. Everything; the meat, the vegetables, the desert. It was also expensive. Having learned gentlemanly conduct from watching my hero Roger Moore on TV, I naturally offered to pay mine and Holly's share and promptly saw most of my week's budget disappear.

We walked from the restaurant to a nightclub. It was smoky and loud and the topless women in suspended cages reminded me of the food I'd just overpaid for. I looked at Holly, a flip book cartoon in the persistent strobe light. She seemed different. Distant. More *fatale* than *femme*. Ominous. I turned down offers of drinks, petrified that any obligation to reciprocate would see my remaining francs disappear.

On the Métro journey back to the hostel I clung to the hope that with such a late night and no doubt some carnal pleasures to come, perhaps Holly had managed to get the next day off. A hope I expressed when we were in her hostel room, finally alone, at 2 a.m.

What followed happened rather quickly. No not 'that'. 'That', it seemed, was never on the agenda. Holly proffered a short explanation as to why she had to work, having already taken too many days off, followed by how difficult it had been to adjust to life in Paris and ended with her telling me she didn't want to go out with me any more. I was dumbfounded. I mumbled a confused defence of the virtues of long-distance relationships and of plans I'd made for the year after she was due to return. My arguments became incrementally poorer and less confident with every word, pause and plea. If you have to use reason and logic to convince someone to go without you, best stop. You'd have a better chance through interpretive dance or the use of hand puppets. As I was all danced out and had forgotten to pack any hand puppets, I stopped. I'd also noticed the camp bed that had been brought in while we'd been out. This was, as the French would say, a *fait accompli*. I looked at my watch. It was 2.15 a.m. In just fifteen minutes I'd gone from staying in a love nest to literally a nest.

I couldn't afford to change my ticket home nor or could I

afford to book into a hotel. Survival mode kicked in. I had no choice but to see this week through, somehow.

Holly told me I could stay on the camp bed till Friday. The routine would remain the same: I would leave when she did in the morning and return after she did in the early evening. The light and any libido were turned off.

I spent the next three days wandering around the city of love feeling even more like one of its outcasts. I scowled my way around the sites; the Eiffel Tower, meh. Sacré-Coeur, overrated. The Louvre, old paintings, big deal. Jardin des Tuileries, it's a big garden, get over it. Arc de Triomphe, can't go on it, doesn't move, don't care.

Also it seemed word of my expulsion from the lovers' club had got around and every doting couple in Paris had come out to mock me. They were everywhere. Every cuddle and devoted gaze was aimed at destroying what little spirit I had left. But while I had a return ticket in my pocket and film in my camera, I was never going to give them the satisfaction. Or her.

I focused on employing my phrase book whenever I could and, perhaps in response to that or acknowledging my pathetic state, far from the cliché, the Parisians were helpful and, dare I say it, friendly.

I spent the evenings smiling through Holly's translations of her friends' witticisms, wondering if I was, in fact, grinning at my own expense. I spent the days sightseeing, taking pictures, eating Le McChicken and mouthing silent cynicisms at every romantic couple that fell into view. 'Yeah, you're happy now but it might be all over by the end of the day. Live it up suckers!'

On my last day, I bade farewell to Holly, bought some

cheese for my parents with my remaining currency (I was still a good Indian boy) and headed back to London.

First loves are always intense affairs. A blank canvas for a painter who has never picked up a brush. Holly was my first love but I was not hers. She was way ahead of me in the experience stakes. I can fully understand her being scared off by my future plans, the ferocity and idealism of a romantic neophyte. But did she have to deliver the fatal blow in Paris? Croydon, Romford, Slough! I could've made a hundred other suggestions. A week earlier or later by letter, phone or carrier pigeon would have been preferable.

A few weeks later I discovered that affable Claude was her new beau. I kept my devastation private.

My relationship with Holly had come to an end, but Paris continued to be offered to me via subsequent relationships and friendships. Any suggestion of revisiting such a graveyard of retrospection were akin to offering me underpants filled with tuberculosis. I successfully avoided Paris for the next two decades.

However, when the invitation came for my wife and I to spend a couple of days in Paris with our close friends Alan and Arlene, it was impossible to turn down. They were and remain two of our favourite people in the world and this was their cherished city.

My first step onto Parisian pavement brought sense memories that hit me like Thor's hammer. I felt momentarily lost, alone and confused once again. My second step steadied me. By my third step I became aware of my wife holding my hand. My fourth step took me out of the fog into the beautiful present.

I think, for the first time in twenty years, I felt sorry for my younger self. I'd had no idea what I was dealing with back then. A lamb to the slaughter. An adult in years but a child in perspicacity.

I think it's important to revisit our younger selves once in a while, our successes, our hurts, our stupidities. To be able to say 'Hey you did good', to put a consoling arm around our younger selves and say 'It'll be all right, you get past this', and to learn from and forgive our failings. Of course it helps if you're surrounded by love when you do.

Paris with Meera, Alan and Arlene was everything I'd always wanted Paris to be. All my fractured romantic notions were reassembled. The famous sites were wonderful, I ate nothing with the prefix 'Mc' and this time I was actually in some of the photos. Alan and Arlene showed us some of their favourite places and haunts, and the whole trip was bathed in the warm glow of fondness and laughter. It became their Paris. Our Paris. Not Holly's Paris.

Any animosity towards Holly had dissipated many years ago. I heard she was happily married with kids. I hope that's still the case. Any relationship, be it a person, a city, a continent, has its positive and negative aspects, but sometimes it's useful to see it through the most loving eyes. Sometimes those aren't your own.

So, Paris . . . *je t'aime* . . . but it took a while.

THE LONG QUEUE

Jennifer Higgie

JENNIFER HIGGIE is a writer and editorial director of *frieze*. Her novel *Bedlam* is based on the nineteenth-century fairy painter Richard Dadd; she is currently adapting it for the screen. Her first children's picture book, *There's Not One*, was released last year. She is also the editor of *The Artist's Joke*.

Last year, I decided it was high time I became British. I had moved to London from Australia twenty years ago and – after lugging a suitcase full of back-issues of the art magazine I work for down to the Home Office in Croydon, queuing for eight hours, convincing a suspicious bureaucrat that I was not and never would be a burden on the state – had been granted indefinite leave to remain. But I never got around to applying for a passport. As a result, I still have to join another long queue – the 'rest of world' one at airports. The people in the EU queue dash past us like joyful sprinters while we shuffle forward like hungry hordes lining up for bread. Once, I stood behind Peter Carey for two hours at Heathrow. He sighed a lot and stared into the distance like someone who had lost something dear to him.

Although I visit Australia every year, and love doing so, it wasn't just the airport queues that prompted my desire for a British passport. I longed to be European, or rather, I longed to be part of the new Europe that had emerged in recent decades: the one that London is, or was, at the heart of. I was born in Vienna in the 1960s. I have no ancestral connections to Austria; my parents were simply living there at the time. In the early 1970s, our home was Paris and my siblings and I went to an international school. Countless languages were spoken, bullying was the stuff of nineteenth-century novels and extreme naughtiness was punished by the brutal withdrawal of mid-morning chocolate. In 1975, my father was posted to the Australian embassy in Belgrade. Back then, Yugoslavia was, of course, communist and we travelled a lot through Eastern Europe. Most weekends, Dad would suggest 'a little round trip'. Mum would pack a picnic, Dad would pass us his 1956 copy of *Europa Touring* and off we'd go. He'd get us to read out loud the history of every village we drove through. The Uruguayan writer Eduardo Galeano famously wrote that: 'Scientists say human beings are made of atoms but a little bird told me that we are also made of stories.' It's not an idea any child would have a problem with.

Travelling between countries in communist Europe back then was thrilling and bleak in equal measure. We passed watchtowers that were so sinister I couldn't believe they were real; Alsatian dogs roamed no-man's land and soldiers waved us across the border with their machine guns. We saw cars searched for stowaways; families just like ours sat waiting on benches, grey-faced with fear. In a gloomy restaurant in Sofia, a waiter sneeringly called Dad a capitalist when he asked if there was anything apart from sausages on offer. From the shores of Lake Ohrid in Macedonia we gazed across towards Albania, a country that sounded like a mad fairy tale: no one could visit it, they had banned Christmas, outlawed the saxophone and loved Norman Wisdom and Chairman Mao in equal measure. Back in Belgrade, my younger brother and I cut eyeholes in the front pages of *Pravda* and loitered in the street, pretending to be American spies. Every couple of months a nice man would come to our home to clear the place of bugs. Not as in insects.

As our parents didn't want us to go a communist school, my sister and I were sent to board in Bexhill-on-Sea. We imagined something from Enid Blyton and we weren't far wrong: there were midnight feasts, pashes and crushes, lacrosse and bad food. Hockey trumped Marxism by miles in that sleepy Sussex town. We were there for two years, most of which I spent mortified at having to wear cardboard-stiff communist jeans when all of the other girls wore Levis. Their eyes went blank when I tried to explain that Mum refused to buy Western clothes on the black market. One summer night I made a bid for freedom. After lights out in the dormitory, with the aid of a pair of scissors, I escaped through the confiscations room window and went to a disco at the local orphanage. I don't recall how I knew about it. As I danced to Abba with those open-minded orphans, no one commented on the cut of my jeans and I felt free. I was caught later that night and exposed as a fraud: someone who had two living parents. My sister, who is much cooler than me, also ran away, but she went to a boys' school. She was caught and came back chastened and kissed.

We used to travel back to Belgrade in our school uniforms as unaccompanied minors. We always flew JAT – the state Yugoslav airline. Our red straw boaters and deep green capes made us feel a little self-conscious, yet as soon as we boarded the aircraft and were greeted in Serbo-Croatian we felt at home. The first time we made the trip, our mother met us at Belgrade airport with our younger brother. He had mysteriously developed an American accent and mocked us for sounding so English. Six months earlier, we had all been Australians. Long before it became fashionable, we children understood that identity was as fluid as you wanted it to be.

When the wall came down and Europe opened its borders, I remembered those watchtowers and felt very glad. A poet had become the president of Czechoslovakia! In 1995, on a balmy evening in Berlin, my friends and I gathered with thousands of people in the grounds of Christo's *Wrapped Reichstag*. The federal parliament loomed above us like a gigantic gift to the future, a symbol of a new Germany, a new Europe, a new era. We talked and drank late into the night and, among the usual nonsense, I recall a sincere celebration of art and freedom. The next day, I bought a fragment of the material that had clad the building to give to my younger brother. He still has it on his desk. As soon as I could, I travelled to Albania. Tirana's great mayor, Edi Rama – now prime minister – had been an artist in Paris but decided to return to his country when communism tumbled. When he was voted in, the first thing he did was to supply free paint to anyone who wanted to brighten up their dingy apartment blocks. The city is now wildly colourful and buskers play their saxophones on street corners.

When I began the long process of applying to become British, the first thing I had to do was to pass the Life in the UK Test. I downloaded the app and began to study. Are there bishops in the House of Lords? When did the Romans leave Britain? What was the Black Death? When I felt that I knew my stuff, I contacted the Home Office and they told me to go to an Iranian Centre in West London to sit the test. I passed. But then Brexit happened and now I've lost the urge to go through with my application. I know I'm jilting my fiancée at the altar, but the thing is, he's changed.

That the UK is – was – part of Europe had lulled me into a sense that the world was getting more civilised; that borders were, if not dissolving, at least getting a little less mean. A lot of my friends and colleagues in London are European. They're artists and writers and curators and gallerists; people who have enriched the cultural life of Britain inestimably. For the first time in two decades, they're asking me how I got my visa. I tell them about Croydon. I warn them about the queues. I give them tips about the Life in the UK app. The other day, an Italian friend laughed wryly and said: 'We're all Australian now.'

GOING BACK

Simon Garfield

A muddy green folder on the desk in front of me contains the story of my family, and the story is familiar and sad. The folder holds about thirty items. I pull them all out at once, a spillage of small photographs and documents with rusting paper clips, but the place to begin is clearly with my dad's typed CV. I'm not sure when it was composed or why, but I wonder if it wasn't just for moments like this.

Herbert Sidney Garfunkel was born in Hamburg on 3 November 1919, two months after Adolf Hitler joined the German Workers' Party. He attended local primary and secondary schools in Hamburg, but in December 1933 his parents decided that the country was no longer a safe place for a fourteen-year-old Jewish boy, and so he was put on a boat to England. He attended the Perse school in Cambridge, and in 1936 was articled as a solicitor to a prominent firm in London.

His training was interrupted by the war, and he served first as an officer in the Durham Light Infantry, and then with an intelligence department of the Allied Expeditionary Force. He had translation duties: his fluent German, which once must have been treated with such suspicion at school, was now used to assist bombing raids against his birthplace. My file contains a handsome certificate of merit with his full title: Lance Corporal Garfield. That was his anglicised name. Without the change I would have been Simon Garfunkel; how terribly difficult in the playground that would have been.

His parents got out too, but only just. The file contains a shipping document for my grandparents' property, four vans' worth, from a London firm of 'wharfingers' specialising in international shipping, with a date of May 1939. I still have an item from that shipment, a small round Biedermeier dining table that must have once hosted nervous tea parties and now displays Cornish ceramics.

My mother suffered a similar dislocation. She was born in the northern German port of Bremerhaven, and in April 1934 she emigrated with her parents to Jerusalem, then under the British mandate in Palestine. She met my father on a trip to London for a wedding in the early 1950s, and they were soon wed themselves, and had my brother Jonathan in 1955 and me five years later. There are some celebratory family photographs from our life in Hampstead Garden Suburb, my father a successful solicitor, my mother an assistant in a nursing home, Germany a long way in the past. One of my earliest memories I can date precisely: my mother screaming at our television as England won the World Cup. That was it for her: utter joy, the final vindication. We bought the commemorative stamps and sent them all over the world.

But the next set of documents are condolence letters – for my father's heart attack when he was fifty-five, my brother's sudden death from a virus he contracted as a doctor when he was twenty-three, and my mother with breast cancer the following year, when she was fifty-four. I was thirteen, eighteen and nineteen. 'Words cannot express . . .' 'How shocked we both were to hear ...' One letter advised me not to consider myself jinxed. Another noted how hard my family had worked to create a new life in a new country, and it was up to me now.

And now I want to add my own document to the file. I want to go back. The day after Brexit I talked to my eldest son, Ben. We were both in shock of course, but he had already found a way forward. We would become Germans again, a personal reunification. We would not be saying goodbye to Europe at all, but becoming greater Europeans; with dual-citizenship, the country that my parents came to fear and loathe we would embrace once more.

Many years before, the German government had offered a scheme whereby the descendants of those who fled the Third Reich could reverse the move – a very personal reparation. You needed as much proof as you could muster – parental birth certificates ideally, but failing that something that placed them in Germany before the Nazis and anywhere else after. I had my father's school reports from Hamburg and Cambridge, I had shipping papers, I had the whole tragic trail. Copies are now lodged with the German embassy in London, and we're waiting on news. I've been told it could take a year, such is the sudden popularity of the scheme.

What would my parents have thought? (They wouldn't drive in a Mercedes or smile for a Leica if they could avoid it, and they would never again holiday in the Schwarzwald.) I think they would have approved, just as I think they would have approved of our recent trips to Berlin to visit the galleries and art squats and Holocaust memorials. They would certainly have cheered Angela Merkel's instinctive welcome towards so many migrants. They would have realised how the world has changed for the worse and for the better, and how even the greatest ruptures may heal with time. They were always for giving.

I've kept my family papers in the same folder for years, and they've never become less painful to look at. But the folder is only part of a larger set of files in a larger box. There's a wallet with my father's speeches – weddings, legal conventions, Jewish lodge meetings. There's another box of photographs: my mother in swimsuit in Israel under a canopy on a beach, her father in his dental whites in Jerusalem, my paternal grandparents at a train station in France – new Europeans finding themselves again, and always smiling for the photos. And then, finally, there is the leather album with congratulatory telegrams marking the marriage of my grandparents at the grand Palast-Hotel in Hamburg, with the very best of views over the Alster, white waiters with their Gewürtztraminer, exactly nine months before the birth of my father. The album is claret and plump, tightly bound at the spine, and there must be at least 200 messages. *'Herzliche glückwünsche sendet.'* *'Es gratulieren herzlich.'* *'Dem neuvermählten paare sendet herzlichste gratulation.'* From Heinz und Grete Hermann, from Alex Silverstein, from Max Katz.

Such a close community, each in each other's phone books, soon to be scattered, never to take anything for granted again. How many, I wonder, now have relatives filing applications with Europe's German embassies? Not nearly enough. The Palast-Hotel is long gone.

A SONG FOR EUROPE

Ian Rankin

IAN RANKIN was born in the Kingdom of Fife in 1960 and graduated from the University of Edinburgh in 1982. He then spent three years writing novels when he was supposed to be working towards a PhD in Scottish Literature. His first Rebus novel was published in 1987, and the Rebus books are now translated into thirty-six languages and are bestsellers worldwide. Ian Rankin has been elected a Hawthornden Fellow, and is also a past winner of the Chandler-Fulbright Award. He is the recipient of four Crime Writers' Association Dagger Awards including the prestigious Diamond Dagger in 2005. In 2004, Ian won America's celebrated Edgar Award for *Resurrection Men*. He has also been shortlisted for the Anthony Award in the USA, won Denmark's Palle Rosenkrantz Prize, the French Grand Prix du Roman Noir and the Deutscher Krimipreis. Ian Rankin is also the recipient of honorary degrees from the universities of Abertay, St Andrews, Edinburgh, Hull and the Open University. A contributor to BBC2's *Newsnight Review*, he also presented his own TV series, *Ian Rankin's Evil Thoughts*. Rankin is a number one bestseller in the UK and has received the OBE for services to literature, opting to receive the prize in his home city of Edinburgh, where he lives with his partner and two sons.

As a child of the 1960s and 70s, growing up in working-class Scotland, what did Europe mean to me? Well, the Second World War mostly, as played out over and over again in comics such as the *Victor*, *Hotspur* and *Commando*. My parents had served in the war and it was still very real to them, while for me it was mythic but no less powerful for that.

What else? Well, we had the *Eurovision Song Contest* (back in the days when we were contenders), and casually racist comedians on TV. Later there was Manuel in *Fawlty Towers*. Oh, and my mother and sister both had a soft spot for Sacha Distel.

That was about it. My mother never cooked anything 'foreign', and holidays meant a caravan in St Andrews or a cheap B&B in Blackpool. Eventually my high school broadened my cultural horizons with summer trips to Germany (when I was sixteen) and Switzerland (two years later). I'd staggered through French and German qualifications, just about scraping passes in each. Then came university – and in the third year I met my girlfriend. She had a wheeze. When I graduated, we should go pick grapes in France. So that's what we did, spending a few months on a vineyard near Castillon-la-Bataille (not too far from Saint-Émilion). As part of the trip, we hitch-hiked around southern France and into Italy, meeting a fascinating array of people who were kindness incarnate. One couple let us hitch a ride on their canal boat for a day (we covered about twelve miles). Another insisted on putting us up for a few nights at their place in Nimes. One of them was a musician and asked in return that we translate a particular Bob Dylan song into French for him.

The summer of 1982 was the start of my love affair with Europe. Yes, the cultures I encountered were very different from the UK, but then the component parts of the UK were subtly (and not so subtly) different from each other too. The people, however . . . well, they were far from alien. They liked music and laughter, were interested in the larger world, surrounded themselves with friends and family, and tried as best they could to get on in the great adventure called life.

We ended that trip with a short stint working in Shakespeare and Company bookshop in Paris, a place I venerated, having read James Joyce's *Ulysses* as an undergraduate. Back in Edinburgh I took stock of everything I'd learned and decided to apply to do a PhD, with Muriel Spark – that most European of Scottish novelists – as my subject. Spark was living in Italy at the time, and had been influenced by the *nouveau roman*. She led me towards further adventures in European writing, though I never did complete my studies – I was too busy trying to write my own novels. I married my girlfriend and we settled in London, until that city started to grind us down. There was only one thing for it: we would move to France. We had no children and didn't need much money: how hard could it be?

Well, French bureaucracy is a thing of harsh beauty and

there were plenty of hazards to be negotiated. But we found a ramshackle house in rolling countryside, sold our flat in Tottenham, and headed off with all our worldly goods. We would eventually stay six full years, during which time Miranda would give birth to both our sons and I would learn some rudimentary French. I would also gain a deeper appreciation of the country, its politics, history and psyche. By the time we left, I was established as a novelist and my books were being translated, meaning trips to other European destinations. My novels were set in contemporary Scotland and took many of their plots from the news headlines, but I began to learn that these various crimes and social issues were not unique to Scotland or even the UK. Xenophobia, social injustice, power politics, commercial corruption – these were themes that resonated in France and Germany and Italy and Greece. No society is crime free, and the crimes encountered in the UK differ little from those found in neighbouring countries. Humans are humans, our sins, failings and foibles recognisable, almost as part of a universal language.

But what of the bigger picture, beyond the world of fiction? The twenty-first century is already more connected, or at least connectable, than ever in history. I can learn at least something of any culture instantly by means of Google. I can communicate with the world without leaving my armchair. News flies at me from all around the globe. But am I better informed than the callow young man who stuck his thumb out on a canal towpath in the south of France? Information is readily available, almost too much to be assimilated; but knowledge, the kind of knowledge that comes with first-hand experience, goes deeper – it becomes hard-wired. Borders, physical and otherwise, are anathema to writers. We want meetings of minds and meetings of flesh and blood. Huge problems are staring us in the face, while others are just around the next bend. Cooperation is the surest way to begin to tackle them. We need to work together, remembering that community trumps adversity.

As a child, when asked to write my address on a school jotter, I started with my street name, then my town and county, then Scotland, followed by the UK, Europe, the World and finally the Universe. That connective tissue is more important to me now than it ever was. I would hate for my sons, and the generations after them, not to share it.

A EUROPEAN PICTURE

Mark Kermode

MARK KERMODE is chief film critic for the *Observer* newspaper. He broadcasts on BBC Radio 5Live and on the BBC News Channel. He is the author of several books on cinema, including *It's Only a Movie*, *The Good, the Bad and the Multiplex* and *Hatchet Job*. He plays double bass in The Dodge Brothers, a skiffle and blues band who work with pianist Neil Brand to provide live accompaniment for silent movies.

As a film-critic who likes to wave the flag for films made in the UK, I've often found myself faced with a thorny descriptive problem; should so-called 'British' movies be referred to as 'European'? Quite apart from worrying about whether particular writers, directors, actors or composers choose to identify as English, Welsh, Scottish or Northern Irish, the question of whether the UK film industry *as a whole* should be included under the European umbrella has always been fraught with contradictions.

In general, if a UK journalist writes about 'European cinema', many of their readers imagine that they are referring to so-called 'foreign language' films, made on the other side of the Channel and distinctly different to our own home-grown fare. Yet ever since the UK joined the EEC in 1973, the things we consider inherently 'British' – including our national cinema – have by definition been an integral part of Europe. More importantly, many of our leading film-makers actively define themselves as 'European'. So why the divide?

The French film-maker François Truffaut once famously quipped that there was a 'certain incompatibility' between the terms 'cinema' and 'Britain'. He was talking to Alfred

Hitchcock about his move from London to Hollywood, and his comments seemed to imply that the director's cinematic genius could only be truly expressed once he had shed the parochial shackles of this green and 'anti-dramatic' land. Although Truffaut was being provocative (one of his own oddest movies, *Fahrenheit 451*, was of course 'a British film'), those words stuck. Over the decades, they have become emblematic of a perceived European snobbery about British movies – the belief that films made in the UK are somehow artistically inferior to those produced across the Channel, or indeed across the Atlantic.

Many critics (myself included) have used Truffaut's words as a stick with which to beat those French film theorists who have looked dismissively down their *Cahiers du Cinéma*-reading noses at the maligned spectre of our indigenous film industry ('Bollocks to Truffaut!' quipped film-maker Stephen Frears). In truth, however, there really is no such thing as a 'British film' *per se*, particularly not in an age in which international co-funding has become the key to film production. Many (if not most) of the films that are popularly considered to be 'home-grown' are made with money that comes from a variety of sources outside of the UK. And while Hollywood continues to rely on British talent and facilities to create their biggest blockbusters (from *Star Wars* to *Harry Potter*), those responsible for making and – exhibiting – the smaller, edgier films which define our national cinema have traditionally looked towards Europe for inspiration.

Although the UK opted out of the Eurimages fund (which arguably made it harder for some small co-productions to get made), films as diverse as Steve McQueen's *Shame*, Andrea

Arnold's *Fish Tank*, Stephen Frears's *Philomena*, Matthew Warchus's *Pride* and Sarah Gavron's *Suffragette* have all in recent years benefitted in varying ways from some form of European-based funding. Read any interview with a film-maker at the cutting edge of UK cinema, and the chances are they will refer to themselves and their work as 'European'. Take as typical these words from Carol Morley, director of *The Falling*, as she prepared to embark upon a film project in the US: 'I've always been fascinated by the films the German emigres made in America, which to me are so very European. Film language is universal, and I hope my films transcend boundaries. But recently I saw someone describe *The Falling* as "weird", so maybe the correct term should be "weird European!"'

This belief that film transcends national boundaries is, of course, nothing new. Take the example of Ken Russell – arguably the greatest British director of the twentieth century. Russell's favourite film-makers were Michael Powell and Emeric Pressburger, the duo behind *A Matter of Life and Death*, *Black Narcissus* and *The Red Shoes*. Together, Powell and Pressburger were known as 'The Archers', and their screen logo (a red, white and blue target pierced with arrows) proudly bore the words 'London England'. Today, an English Heritage blue plaque marks the flat in Gloucester Place where the two worked together. They couldn't be *more* British.

Except, of course, Pressburger was Hungarian. And from an aesthetic point of view, there was little about The Archers' output which fitted the clichéd view of 'British cinema' in the post-war period. When Ken Russell wrote his autobiography, he slyly named it *A British Picture* – an ironic phrase which his mother would reportedly use to describe the drab home-grown fare of which she was less than enamoured. ('Is it a *British* picture?' she would ask with disdain). Yet The Archers' movies were awash with colour, music and fantastical invention, pushing at the boundaries of the cinematic form – bold, adventurous and expressionist.

Russell himself made films as stylistically revolutionary as those of Powell and Pressburger. With *Women in Love*, *The Music Lovers*, *The Devils* and *Tommy*, he put paid to Truffaut's claim that there was anything 'incompatible' about Great Britain and Great Cinema. His horizons were international (Fellini once told him that 'they call me the Italian Ken Russell') and his sensibilities knew no boundaries. Yet Russell was also quintessentially British – part of a brilliantly unruly tradition which would continue through the work of Nicolas Roeg, Ben Wheatley, Lynne Ramsay, Carol Morley, Danny Boyle, et al.

This lineage is often counterpointed with the work of directors like Ken Loach and Mike Leigh, whose films are frequently viewed as being more in synch with the 'kitchen sink' traditions that flourished in UK theatre, film and television in the fifties and sixties, and are therefore seen as more 'typically' British. Yet both Loach and Leigh have long been recognised as great European film-makers, and both have significantly won applause on the Continent – even when the plaudits sometimes faltered at home. Both have won the prestigious Palme d'Or prize at the Cannes Film Festival in France, Loach having earned that honour twice, for *The Wind That Shakes the Barley* and more recently for *I, Daniel Blake*.

Both look to Europe for funding and inspiration (Leigh cites Ermanno Olmi's Italian neorealist classic *The Tree of Wooden Clogs* as one of his favourite films of all time), and both are part of a cultural tradition that is *both* British and European. As Loach's long-time producer Rebecca O'Brien said in Cannes in 2016, on the eve of the Brexit vote, 'I feel quite strongly that the way that the European film community can and does work together in terms of co-productions is a really good example of how Europe can work. There is a British tendency to look across the Atlantic to make films and that seems to be a money-driven operation. Whereas in Europe, cultural and important stories like ours can be told.'

As for Danny Boyle, long before he rose to fame as the director of such stylishly expressionist fare as *Trainspotting* he produced the ground-breaking TV short *Elephant* for director Alan Clarke. The apotheosis of a particularly gritty form of UK TV and cinema, Clarke would be a guiding light for Boyle and also for Ben Wheatley – British directors whose films draw on the social realist traditions associated with Clarke, but also upon the avant-garde sensibilities so rarely found in mainstream American movies, but so fundamental to the evolution of European cinema.

Whatever the economic and political ramifications of Brexit (and as a diehard Remainer, my hopes are not high), few artists working within the UK film industry are likely to take the isolationism of our withdrawal from the EU to heart. They know that British cinema has long been a part of a rich European tradition which has made our national cinema stronger, brighter and more independent than ever. Just as there is nothing incompatible about the words 'Britain' and 'cinema', so there is no artistic boundary between Britain and Europe. Our cinema is European – it always has been, and it always will be. Nothing will change that.

FOLDING BROWN PAPER

Amy Liptrot

AMY LIPTROT is a writer who grew up on a sheep farm in Orkney, Scotland. Her memoir, *The Outrun* (2016), was a *Sunday Times* bestseller, Radio 4 Book of the Week, won the Wainwright Book Prize for nature and travel writing and the PEN Ackerley Prize for memoir. She is a trained journalist, lifelong diarist and outdoor swimmer. She has lived in many places across Europe but is currently found in West Yorkshire.

The German term '*wanderjahr*', or journeyman year, refers to the tradition of setting out to travel after completing an apprenticeship as a craftsman. Three years ago, my first book written but not yet published, I left Scotland and embarked on a nomadic period. In that year I lived in a London tower block, a Greek island bookshop and various Berlin tenements. Unencumbered by a mortgage or children, I exploited cheap air travel and the freedom to move and work within the EU.

I worked in Greece, one of the poorest countries in Europe, where the people who worked in the tourist gift shops in the summer were unemployed for the rest of the year, and everyone from the town had sold up and moved to the city and their former homes made into hotels. And I lived in one of the richest countries, Germany, where government benefits were generous and refugees accepted. I moved freely between these countries with just enough euros in my bank account.

In Berlin I was broke and, through friends, found work in the warehouse of a company that imported and sold high end speciality tea. Our job was to pack the tea by hand into individual bags. We dealt with sacks of fragrant tea and flowers: white and jasmine tea from China, Assam and Darjeeling from India, green tea from Japan, dried roses and lavender and ginger. We weighed it on scales like drug dealers, and packed it with our hands in surgical gloves, sometimes wearing dust masks. The tea sold, in a smart store in the middle of the city, for prices high enough to justify paying us Germany's minimum wage, rather than exporting the jobs to the developing world.

Everyone that worked there was, like me, from elsewhere and living in the city to pursue creative ambitions. The others were musicians, painters, photographers and artists. We represented a subculture in Berlin of Western twenty- and thirty-somethings who had chosen not to have regular work, who had chosen uncertainty and were privileged to do so. We were a highly educated bunch of factory workers, international wannabes thinking of other things. Not coming back after the weekend was a victory, a colleague didn't turn up and we wondered hopefully if he'd sold a painting.

Many of us found the repetitive work soothing. It was reassuring to have a well-defined task with a start and end time, rather than the subjective challenges of trying to make art. For orderly, productive days, I weighed tea and folded paper bags and stuck labels. I listened to podcasts about the sleeping patterns of animals, about foghorns and heartbreak, about the political mood in Greece and surrogate mothers in Thailand. I folded hundreds of pieces of brown paper as the day passed; the sky moved from grey to black and my mood changed from calm to anxious. I could have gone anywhere in the world, I thought, and here I was spending my days in an industrial estate in suburban Berlin in cold January, folding brown paper.

While we were weighing and folding and sticking, we

talked. I had conversations with fellow tea packers about the impossibility of true translation, about methods of international smuggling, about grants for artists, while stapling thousands of tea bags to pieces of card, while weighing 51g quantities of dried flowers into crisp brown bags. The Polish artist told me that in seven years of living in Berlin she hadn't learned German, and thus was defended from news and society and advertising and could concentrate on her art. A Canadian painter told me about his studio, rented cheaply from property developers who wanted to give their newly built apartments a desirable, arty edge.

The warehouse was a microcosm of the EU. The staff represented a cross section of Europe and the Anglophone world. Serbians and Australians, Brits and Spaniards. I pitied the Americans their complex visa application processes and appointments with expensive lawyers, all with an uncertain outcome, at the whim of an immigration officer.

We didn't have guaranteed hours but this suited us. We could drop the job as easily as it could drop us. It was casual work. We had casual relationships. It was a casual city. We were having sexual adventures in the Eurozone. I was not so much an economic immigrant as a lifestyle immigrant, coming here seeking new experiences.

In Berlin, where reminders of terrible history were everywhere – the bronze cobblestones, Stolpersteine, on every street bear the names of Jewish people taken from the houses – it was easy to see why a peaceful union of nations makes sense. Although I come from its very fringe – I grew up on a cliff looking west to the Atlantic, the setting sun and America – I am a proud European. The borders of Europe, at Calais and the northern coasts of the Mediterranean, hold back refugees trying to enter the countries I have been freely moving between. The luck of the passport I hold allows a lifestyle many risk their lives for. I am so fortunate to have lived in these times.

Smoking on my balcony at 1 a.m., thinking about returning to the UK, I hear wild geese passing high above. The migrating animals don't know about national borders. I left the tea warehouse but have retained excellent abilities to fold brown paper and weigh precise amounts. I declare myself a citizen of Scotland and the internet and the sea.

POST EXIT STRESS DISORDER

Nicci Gerrard and Sean French

NICCI GERRARD was educated in Worcestershire and Oxford. After working in a children's home, she founded the feminist journal *Women's Review*. From 1990 she worked as a literary editor and feature writer for the *Observer,* among other subjects covering the trials of Rosemary West, Harold Shipman, and Ian Huntley and Maxine Carr. She has published six novels. Since 1997 she has written psychological thrillers with her husband, Sean French, under the name Nicci French.

SEAN FRENCH was educated in London and Oxford. He worked as a journalist on the *Sunday Times*, *New Society* and the *New Statesman*. He has published various books, including biographies of Patrick Hamilton and Brigitte Bardot, and three novels. He and Nicci Gerrard have four grown-up children and live in London and Suffolk.

Nicci Gerrard

We were in Sweden for midsummer – a time of new greenness, enduring light, ribbons round the maypole and garlands in the hair – and for the results of the referendum. My mother was with us: old, frail, disabled and registered blind, she had been a rather eccentric one-woman Remain campaigner in the small town where she lives. Through the night that never got quite dark, I woke repeatedly to see what was happening, at first to confirm me in my optimism and then to confirm me in my despair.

At five, I got out of bed and went for a run in a world that was still green, still full of light, but felt entirely changed. I swam in the lake instead of taking a shower and then I called each of my four twenty-something children in turn. They were, in their different ways, utterly desolate. I remember squeezing my eyes half-closed as I talked to them and pressing the phone hard against my face: I wanted to be able to say something that would make it less bad. That's what mothers do. *I'm so sorry*, I kept saying. I felt obscurely ashamed.

Parents want and expect to hand on a better world. Whatever good things we've inherited from our own parents, we want to give our children more. More opportunities, more adventures, more happiness, wider horizons: more of the world.

141

I'm fifty-nine years old. I've been able to work in Europe and travel without constraints. I've been able to buy property cheaply and see it soar in value, my individual worth doubling through absolutely no efforts or merits of my own. I've got a pension comfortably ticking away ready for when I retire. And although a passionate Remainer (I didn't know quite how passionate, I admit, until the result of the referendum), I am part of the segment of the UK population that largely voted to leave and I feel a kind of collective guilt. We've said to the generations beneath us: you will not able to have those things we had. There will be jobs you will not be able to apply for, cities you won't live in, friends you will not make, love affairs and marriages you won't have. There will be borders to your lives that you will find it harder to cross.

And if they are less able to be citizens of Europe, citizens of Europe will of course be less able to be citizens of the UK – the country that I still believe is tolerant, inclusive, stoical and kind, but is having a kind of mid-life crisis.

One of my daughters is a teacher in a primary school in north London. Her young students come from dozens of different countries, including Poland, Hungary, Albania, Greece, Sweden, Romania, Spain, Italy, Bulgaria, the Netherlands, Switzerland, Ireland ... They are first, second and third generation. Many of them arrive in her class unable to speak English and by the end of the year they are fluent, part of the great democracy of the very young. Another of my daughters is a junior doctor in London's East End. Her colleagues come from all corners of the globe and so do her patients. She was working in a hospital in South Africa at the time, and for months after she felt she no longer wanted to return to her own country: home no longer had the same meaning for her. The fabric of the NHS is made up of people who come from all over the world. Now that fabric will be ripped. A third daughter has a part-time job on a cheese stall in London's Borough Market (in 2017 the target of a terrorist attack in which people of all cultures and creeds and races came together to stand together and support each other). Her colleagues are two Italians (one of whom is married to a Russian woman), a Bulgarian and a Hungarian. My son quite recently worked for the best part of a year in Berlin, alongside other young people from all over Europe (and my nephew still lives in that city). And my children seem fairly typical of their urban generation, where identity is not so fixed, where notions of belonging are not so limiting and where borders are porous. Not so much 'them', not so much 'us' and more of a 'we': a short word meaning collective humanity.

They are also, perhaps because they are young and full of energy and purpose, more optimistic than I find myself to be as we travel towards the edge of this great change (and I have always thought of myself as a wilful optimist, to the point of stupidity). When I spend time with them and their friends, I feel more hopeful as well. Great changes happen, epic shifts like the tectonic plates buckling, but within these there are small groups and movements that bit by bit, drop by drop, make a difference to what the world looks like. My Borough Market daughter told me how, shortly after the referendum, she was in a pub with friends and one of them – from Eastern Europe – was insulted by an ignorant stranger all fired-up by the result with a sense of self-righteous, vindictive triumph. She and most of the other people who were witnesses rallied round to protect her friend. We were complacent before the result and now we are not. To be inclusive, to be tolerant and welcoming and kind, these are not passive things but active and dynamic, no longer to be taken for granted but to be fought for and protected.

It sometimes feels we're living through a creeping kind of civil war, people lining up on either side of the divide, for and against, old and young, urban and rural, a great rift splitting the country and an ill wind blowing through it. I turn off the radio when I hear the resentful, bellicose voices, the discussions that aren't discussions at all because the language of doubt – which is the language of humanity – has been extinguished. I read the paper with a kind of dread. Toxic times. But I don't usually feel like that when I'm with the younger generations because from them I am learning about a new language of hope and of change, and also having my notion of home, hospitality and family bolstered. Robert Frost's statement about home has been much quoted and misquoted as the place 'where, when you have to go there, / They have to take you in.' But I think that home is where you *want* to let people in and that family is as large as you chose it to be. Sean and I used to read and reread the great Tove Jansson's Moomintroll books to the children. Delightful, odd, a bit mystical, they are about what it is to be curious, fearful and in need of family, whatever family means. Moominmamma always says that if a guest arrives, you just lay another place at the table. I'm with Moominmamma: open the door, put out another knife and fork.

It is the young who are showing me how to be optimistic again. And it is the young in whom I am placing my faith. Our generation and the ones above have snatched too much away from them. (I've taken to incoherently chanting Bob Dylan's great anthem. 'The Times They Are A-Changin', especially the verse that tells older people that their 'road is / Rapidly agin'. / Please get out of the new one / If you can't lend your hand'.) That morning after in Sweden, Sean's relatives kept saying to us: *What have you done? What on earth have you done?* When I called our children, I said the same to them: *What have we done?* By 'we' I didn't mean them. I wanted to comfort them, but in the end, they comforted me more. *It will be all right.* Maybe. In the fragile, febrile world we've created, I plant my flag on their soil.

Sean French

Am I British? Really? That's what it says on my passport. I was born in Bristol. I've lived most of my life in London and Suffolk. I went to school and university here. This is where I've worked, where I got married, where my children were born and grew up. I studied English literature at school and university. If I feel patriotic, it's for the Britain of Chaucer and Spenser and Shakespeare and Milton. For our parish churches, the Book of Common Prayer, the King James Version of the Bible, commemorating a religion I don't believe in.

The boundaries of the English literature I studied were never quite secure, however carefully they were policed, however high the wall. The earliest text we studied, *Beowulf*, was a work whose citizenship status was highly dubious: not written in English and probably not written in Britain. The question of Ireland and Irish writers in so-called English literature was a whole subject in itself, nagging away at our national subconscious. Was Ireland part of Britain or somewhere we were occupying? Edmund Spenser wrote his great (and greatly troubled) patriotic epic, *The Faerie Queene*, while living in Ireland as a civil servant and advocating a policy of genocide that the SS would have approved of. Four centuries later, Samuel Beckett was asked if he was an English writer and replied: '*Au contraire*.' But he was still a part of the English literature course, along with Yeats and Joyce.

I'm a bit like that myself. My paternal grandfather's family was Irish. They came over to Liverpool in the late nineteenth century. Somewhere I have a copy of my great-grandfather's wedding certificate. My great-grandmother signed her name with a cross. It was a typical immigration story. My great-grandfather was a docker with a hole in his head from where a crate fell on him. My grandfather left school at thirteen and when he retired he was a divisional manager in an insurance company. His son (my father) went to Oxford.

My grandparents were rather ashamed of their Irish heritage. They called their two sons Colin and Philip and were appalled when their first two grandchildren were named Sean and Patrick. Why expose what they had gone to such trouble to conceal?

My mother is Swedish. My parents met as postgraduates studying at the University of Indiana in Bloomington in the mid-1950s and then moved back to London. My mother still lives in the first house they bought, in Kentish Town, in 1964. She worked as a translator and a French teacher (yes, yes, I know, Mrs French the French teacher, who happens to be Swedish). London is her home and where she feels at home.

But she still has a Swedish passport, and though she speaks perfect English it is still with a noticeable Swedish accent.

I have no relatives that I know of in Ireland. I haven't met an English relative beyond my immediate family since I was a child. But Sweden is an entirely different matter. My mother has three sisters, who stayed in Sweden and all have families. I'm close to all of them, the living and the dead: grandparents, uncles, aunts, cousins, second cousins, second step-cousins, cousins once removed and cousins' partners, cousins' ex-partners, cousins' ex-partners' children with their new partners.

We meet up every summer for crayfish parties and birthday parties. We meet at New Year and have a sauna on New Year's Eve and jump through a hole in the ice. We meet at funerals. But do I actually feel Swedish? It's not an easy question to answer. I just tried to remember the people I was at school with who had a foreign parent. I can quickly recall German, French, Australian, American, Irish, Polish, South African, Indian, Pakistani, Cypriot parents and – this being north London – many children of Jewish immigrants from Eastern Europe. I can't claim any exotic privilege. While I can speak Swedish, it's when I'm in Sweden that I start to feel English. I love Sweden. But when I'm there I miss the grunginess, the noise, the messiness of London.

But that's not the point. Henry James talks somewhere of life being a mass of connections and associations that begin in the family and end nowhere. This is not the place to discuss the details of Britain leaving the European Union, arguments about democratic accountability (or lack of accountability), of national attachments and supranational attachments. I'm more interested in it as a state of mind. I've spent much of my life immersed in the literature and culture of Britain. One constant is that people have always been complaining about the foreigners. They've always been worrying about the English language itself, corrupted by the importation of foreign words, jargon, Americanisms.

But we are the foreigners. We're the foreigners who earlier foreigners worried about and are now worrying about other later foreigners. The language we're using to worry about them is itself a bastardisation of Old English and Norman French that resolved itself into an unrespectable vernacular spoken in the south-east of England. We can Leave but we can't leave.

When I was younger, I sometimes thought about becoming a dual national of Sweden alongside my UK citizenship. Or perhaps I just thought of it as something slightly strange that was available to me. The reasons I didn't included simple inertia and the fact that it had no point. The only result I was aware of was that I would be liable to do military service in Sweden. In due course, with the apparent end of the Cold War, Sweden phased conscription out. Now it's being brought back. Putin's Russia has recently been conducting military exercises around the Baltic area. They have been pressuring Sweden to allow them a military base on the island of Gotland (which would be rather like allowing Russia a military base on the Isle of Wight). To adapt the words of Karl Kraus, we may not be interested in Europe but Europe is interested in us.

Now my brothers and I are planning to apply for Swedish citizenship for real. There are complicated forms to fill in (in Swedish). You can't do it online. You have to go to the Swedish embassy and convince them in person. There probably won't be any practical benefits for us, apart from avoiding the Other Passports queue at European airports. It's not for the Aquavit and the fermented fish. We've got access to that already. It may just be of some benefit to our children, part of a generation who have grown up seeing Europe as just one single enticing, endlessly various country stretching from Scotland to the Black Sea. They might be able to live and work a bit more easily in Copenhagen or Naples or Marseilles (to name a few cities that are so much a part of our history that we've given them English names).

Even if all we have to show for it is a passport in a language that nobody outside Scandinavia can understand, it will be something to brandish, a symbolic, melancholic, private way of remaining.

WHAT IF BRITAIN WERE TO DISAPPEAR TOMORROW?

Rob Temple

ROB TEMPLE is a journalist and author of the Very British Problems books and social media accounts, which currently have a combined 3.4 million followers on Twitter (@SoVeryBritish), Facebook and Instagram. Born in Peterborough, he now lives in Cambridge, has gradually gone down to no sugars (from two) and owns the UK's largest collection of waterproof jackets, he imagines.

More Brits said 'no, thanks, we really must be off' than 'yes please, that would be lovely' when asked if the UK should leave the EU. So here we are, standing in the hall in our coats, trying to work out how to settle up and actually vacate.

Like all Very British Problems, it's a complicated, messy and awkward situation in which to find ourselves. It makes you wonder if it would be easy to just stop existing altogether, move Britain to the Moon to avoid causing any more fuss.

But if Britain were to just disappear from Earth tomorrow in a puff of kettle steam, what about it might be missed?

Weather

Yes, other countries have weather, but do they discuss it as much as in Britain?

We can take the fact that it's not raining, but just a bit grey, and the fact that it might rain later but also might continue not to rain, and turn it into the most boring but somehow comforting discussion of all time. We have this conversation with everyone we meet on every day of our adult lives.

When the sun shines brightly or the rain falls heavily, we

will transfer this discussion to the front pages of our national papers. When the wind blows strongly enough to bend a tree, we give that wind a human name. When it snows a bit, we will send all our news reporters to stand in it with a microphone while all our trains fall to bits. We have fifty different names for 'a bit chilly' and are unable to dress appropriately for most of the year. When it drizzles we stand outside and burn sausages.

If there was no Britain, mild weather conditions would simply go unnoticed and probably die out as a result, causing havoc.

Tea

Yes, other countries drink tea, but does any other country bang on about this hot, leafy water quite like Brits?

Consuming 165 million daily, tea is a religion for the British, the electric kettle the most worshipped gadget in the land. Consequently, we've developed an intricate set of commandments surrounding the drink's consumption.

Start a new job and mess up the tea round and you'll soon be unemployed again. Say no to a cuppa and it's as if you've just taken a wee on your host's table. Make tea too weak and you're a weirdo; make it too strong, you're a show-off.

Enter a debate about whether milk should go in first or last and you'll end up in a fight to the death. Whole essays have been written on this last issue, which George Orwell called 'one of the most controversial points of all'. And we haven't even started on biscuits.

Get rid of Britain and tea will become just a warm drink

for quenching thirst, rather than a controversial, fussy, argumentative pot of disputed rules and regulations. Who wants that?!

Queues

Yes, other countries queue, but do they treat it as a national sport?

To a Brit, a queue is a minefield. If someone has pushed in, we'll tut, frown, find unity in the eye rolls of others and whisper 'unbelievable' at a non-audible volume. If we desire an extreme adrenaline rush, we might even say something.

Someone queuing slightly to the side of us? Uncertainty over whether someone is actually in the queue or just standing near it? A sign saying 'queue both sides'? All enough to induce a nervous breakdown.

What will we stand in line for? Anything (apart from at a bar, but that's too complicated to go into here). We especially excel at airports, where a Brit will often join a queue without even really knowing what it's for.

With no Britain, queuing wouldn't be nearly such a tense or potentially violent pastime. Wouldn't that be a shame?

Brits Abroad

Yes, other countries go on holiday, but who travels with such grace, charm and curiosity as the Brit?

With a suitcase stuffed with Marmite, factor 4, socks/sandals, wine gums and terrible thrillers, plus a firm grasp of the phrases 'erm, frites?' and 'grande beer, gracias?', we jet off, relaxed from a morning of airport drinking, to crisp ourselves on sunny shores.

We wobble, topless, into air-conditioned supermarkets to stock up on little cans of Estrella to stuff in the minibar fridge.

We amble around museums, hands behind backs so everyone knows we're appreciating the exhibits, and pretend to read the descriptions (fifteen seconds is usually enough).

We describe the most breathtaking structures as 'not bad', then have a Calippo.

If not for Britain, hotels, resorts and tourist spots wouldn't need nearly as many warning signs. A disaster waiting to happen, surely?

Keeping Calm and/or Carrying On

Yes, other countries get angry, but can they suppress it like Britain?

We are a land of letter writers, TripAdvisor reviewers and email complainers. In the sober, public light of day, most of us express anger through the medium of tuts, arm folding, head shakes, mutterings of 'you're welcome' and gritted teeth.

We become so furious that we beg someone for their pardon, before going home to weed the hell out of the garden. We communicate to our fellow Brits that we're the most livid we've ever been by telling them we're 'fine, honestly'. We bellow 'good morning!' at the neighbour who spends all night drilling. We only truly let it all out when safely cocooned in cars.

What would Europe be without this loveable hidden anger to keep everyone guessing? Pretty boring, no?

Apologising

Yes, every country says sorry, but does any country say it so often and meaninglessly as Britain? Sorry, but no.

In Britain, 'sorry' means: 'hello'; 'I didn't quite hear that'; 'I heard that but I'm annoyed'; 'get out of my way'; and, rarely, 'I apologise'.

When a Brit uses the word sorry to actually apologise, it's to inanimate objects: mostly cupboard doors.

Brits apologise when wronged; for instance, if you ram a supermarket trolley into a Brit's leg at 30mph, the Brit will say sorry before limping away to die in the cheese aisle. We'll also apologise for entering a lift, for informing someone that they've dropped something, when someone occupies our reserved seat, for being tired or for walking through a door.

Why? No idea, sorry. But wouldn't it be a shame if we didn't?

Sports, Culture, Inventing/Making Stuff, Science, etc.

Some notable achievements, according to Wikipedia.

So, if Britain were to disappear tomorrow, would the rest of Europe miss us? Actually, having read back all of the above, probably best not to think about it. Sorry.

A PIECE OF THE CONTINENT

Afua Hirsch

AFUA HIRSCH is an award-winning author, journalist and barrister. She has covered legal affairs for the *Guardian* and was its first correspondent for West Africa. She was also the social affairs editor for *Sky News*, and regularly appears on broadcast current affairs debate shows across broadcasters. Before that she practised law as a human rights barrister. Her first book, *Brit(ish)*, is about Britishness and identity, and will be published in January 2018 by Jonathan Cape.

I remember the first time I heard an American talking about 'Europe'. It was 1999, and I was a fresher, at a university trying to ramp up its income by stuffing the undergraduate ranks with American visiting students. These earnest overseas teenagers had the privilege of sitting on the same long benches, or sometimes cross-legged on the floor, and eating the same mushy carrots for which we paid far, far less. They weren't fazed though, they were so excited to be 'in Europe'. What a strange thing to say, I thought. Concerned as I was with the perennial puzzle of being both black and, officially at least, British, it had never occurred to me to feel European as well.

Growing up with mixed heritage, I had an acute sense of the connectedness of different cultures and races, but didn't belong easily to any. My father's father came to the UK in 1939, a few months too old for kindertransport but still only a teenager, following the same route as his fellow Jewish-German child refugees but travelling alone. But I am neither Jewish nor German. My mother's family came to the UK in 1961 from Ghana, as the post-imperial fallout from the first African ex-British colony imploded around them. But I had never lived in Ghana, and cannot speak my mother's mother tongue. I grew up in Wimbledon, a place that bestowed on me a privileged start in life and a middle-class English accent, as well as a physical and psychological distance from any of London's vibrant black communities, the closest of which were a few miles away. Not 'a proper black person' – I was often told – not Jewish, not German. Not British either, if Britishness – as was so often implied – meant white.

A few years later, studying at the Bar, another encounter prompted a search for the European in me. I had managed to land a room in Lincoln's Inn – one of four Inns of Court which greedily cloister away some of the most prime real estate in London, secreting great lawns and magnificent halls behind the innocuous brick of Chancery Lane. The Inn educates its new members about its history with a little booklet you receive on joining, explaining how, for example, renovation in the 1480s was financed by increasing fines for fornicating with women on the premises. It explained too that one of the English language's most famous poems was inspired by the Inn's chapel bell, tolled in mourning for each member who passed away. 'No man is an island' wrote John Donne in 1624, while chaplain at the Inn. 'Every man / is a piece of the continent, a part of the main; / if a clod be washed away by the sea, Europe / is the less . . .'

That poem spoke to me because I had spent my life wanting to be part of the main. By that time – perhaps not surprisingly, given my own family's experience of escaping genocide on one side and authoritarianism on the other – by the time I was at Lincoln's Inn, I was hell-bent on becoming a human rights lawyer. As I listened to Donne's bell tolling, I steeped myself in the history and content of European human rights traditions. As I studied these legal conventions, I experienced something like patriotism for the first time. I felt proud of the fact that Britain conceived of these protections – the right to life, liberty, protection from torture and a fair trial. British people – Winston Churchill among them – played a key role drafting and advocating these standards, creating a new global system, based – in theory at least – on norms.

If my British identity was informed by a sense of belonging in the human rights community, then it was a fragile identity indeed. The anti-human rights act sentiment that existed then, in the mid-2000s, is a direct antecedent of the anti-European sentiment that exists today. The newspapers of the day railed against 'European judges', angered that such diverse villains as prisoners, Muslim clerics and asylum seekers were all entitled to basic levels of humane treatment. The enemies of these rights were disinterested in the fact they originated in the need to prevent a repeat of Nazi atrocities. The EU – which is separate from the human rights organisation the Council of Europe – has a similar genesis. 'There is no hope for the safety and freedom of Western Europe except by the laying aside forever of the ancient feud between the Teuton and the Gaul', Churchill had said in 1953. Otherwise forgiving of Churchill's problematic past – which includes enthusiastic white supremacism and a hatred of Indians – on this, the patriotic enemies of Europe were content to dismiss the old war general. And on 23 June 2016, they won the day.

You don't have to be a human rights lawyer to instinctively feel what is being lost. 'They are talking about going back to 1973, I remember 1973,' one man I interviewed in the run-up to the referendum told me, incredulous. 'As a black man, it was not unusual to have Teddy boys chasing you down the street, calling you names. We were not safe. The EU has given us more protection – not just from racists, but from right-wing British governments as well. What black person in their right *mind*,' he continued, 'wants to go back to 1973?'

Brexit claims to offer a new vision of the future, but it really is about competing views of the past. The nostalgia that characterised the referendum campaign does not afflict everyone equally. One person's joy at 'reclaiming sovereignty' is another's sense of being left vulnerable, at the mercy of British governments with a poor track record on protecting minorities. One person's 'turning to the Commonwealth', is for people like me – whose family is still recovering from the legacy of empire – a celebration of imperial-era exploitation.

'Where do we stand?' Churchill had asked in 1953, of Britain's relationship with Europe. 'We are with them, but not *of* them. We have our own Commonwealth and Empire.'

It was this speech – with all its smug neo-imperialism – that Boris Johnson echoed, finally coming out in favour of Brexit, saying Britain would contribute to, rather than be inside, the EU. The irony is that, just like that autumn day in 1999 when I met the American visiting students, I never really felt *of* Europe until I saw it, diminished, as Britain slips away. Sometimes the strongest identities are those you don't appreciate until they are gone.

IN THE HEAT OF THE SUN

Sarah Winman

SARAH WINMAN grew up in Essex and now lives in London. She attended the Webber Douglas Academy of Dramatic Art and went on to act in theatre, film and television. She has written three novels, *When God was a Rabbit*, *A Year of Marvellous Ways* and *Tin Man*.

In the summer of 1958, my parents drove down to the south of France on their Lambretta. They were twenty-four years old. One can surmise they were deeply in love. This was a well-polished story, set in family folklore and often told at the end of a party or Christmas gathering. It transformed my parents into the carefree adults they once were, when freedom and adventure lay ahead. They took the ferry across the Channel, then wound down through France until they hit Marseille, and then, basically, turned left along the Mediterranean coastline, dazzled by the perfect blue sea and perfect blue sky that accompanied them to Agay.

As a child, this story represented something exotic to me – snapshots of grilled octopus, a Jean Seberg haircut, beach volleyball – and whenever it was brought out and polished one more time, I claimed the experience, determined, one day, to make it mine.

I was seventeen when I finally made the train journey south, eager to test my parents' veracity, to see whether their memory held up to my scrutiny – 1982 was the year I stood on that baking yellow sand.

The winter before, I'd written to estate agents in Fréjus and Saint-Raphaël requesting a flat for the month of August.

I marvel now at how slow the process was. A week for the letter to arrive, a week for the listings to be sent back. The stilted conversation on the telephone in French when a flat was located, finally a banker's draft in francs for a week's deposit that my father said I would never see again.

On arrival, I expected nothing but got everything. A large two-bedroom white stone palace that overlooked the main promenade and beach. It was filled with light. I filled it with friends. I have never lived in anything so spacious since.

I remember, vividly, a slowing down on those first mornings. A whisper from the sun to rise and I crept out from the apartment and traversed the pure morning light till the sand felt cool under my feet. The sound of waves. The occasional shadow of a runner pounding the promenade above. Swallows claimed the sky. I was in thrall to this scene, and I imagined life to be OK.

I used to swim out to a floating platform anchored a little way from shore. I was almost always alone in that early hour, and I'd look back to a town not yet fully awake. It was a beautiful solitude. The heat of the sun just beginning to break through and rest on my skin. Cafes filled up slowly. The faint sound of music rippled. The jagged glare of light on the metal tabletops.

I didn't know what I wanted to do with my life then. I was compliant and hidden, frightened that the great passions others embraced would pass me by. I walked a path laid down by my parents and teachers and it would be another two years before drama school breached that impasse and introduced me to a level of self-examination and curiosity that would remain thereafter. But out there, with a vast horizon to my back, under an ozone layer still thought to be intact, my skin turned a colour it had never been before, and my body spoke, and the sun burnt off that melancholy haze.

When the drinks sellers sold out and emptied their coolers, we took the boxes up to the flat and filled them with watermelon and ice and joined the *beignet* sellers down on the sand. We made friends, made good money. The cash bought dinner and wine for everyone and stock for the next day. We languished in this commune. I grew in ease amid this summer purpose, and threw away my shoes and claimed the pavements and beaches barefoot. I came to know the pulse of the town. Whether it was true or imagined is irrelevant. It was a place of my own creation where I could leave behind my history, my language and build something new. My body unfurled in this preening landscape, and the bare-chested tap dancer who storied his way around the streets became my Bojangles.

The ambient sighs of the breeze, the limpid waters, the smell of my skin, the vivid bougainvillea and oleander, the boulangerie that baked throughout the night that became my night's ending. Sun-ripened apricots and tomatoes. *Saucisson*. *Camembert*. French wine. All these were a first. There was no longer ordinary and mundane. Life had acquired taste.

At night, we gathered on the sand with bottles of wine and water, our conversation lit by stars and cigarettes. At seventeen I still dated boys, but knew this wasn't the whole story. I was scared of the whole story. So, boyfriends came and went, and tan lines became maps, sharp and vivid in the moonlight as the summer wore on.

An afternoon swim out to the raft was where I met her. I never knew her name and barely spoke to her but she was the alternative to the young man swimming at my side, that I knew. We looked at one another and the sea acquired a sudden chill. I swam back to the shore, his incessant chat deafened by the pounding in my ears, my heart? I turned. Her looking at me. I swam on, turned. Her looking. I had found my other story in that swim from shore.

It was five weeks in all, but occupies time more suited to years. The ease and entitlement of long-distance travel hadn't become mainstream then and for many – myself included – plane travel was often price prohibitive. Europe was the scene of our discovery. The Magic Bus taking days to hit the Greek mainland, water bottles emptied and refilled with urine. French interrailing, or coaches that blitzed across autobahns, windscreen wipers struggling against snow. But though so commonplace now, these were still journeys of discovery, of triumph, where we honed our independence and became a more imaginative version of ourselves.

A VERY BRITISH BLINDING

Sunny Singh

SUNNY SINGH was born in Varanasi, India, and brought up in various Indian cantonment towns, Islamabad, Pakistan and New York City. She studied at Brandeis University, Jawaharlal Nehru University, and University of Barcelona, and has worked in Mexico, Chile and South Africa. She is the author of the novels *Nani's Book Of Suicides*, *With Krishna's Eyes* and *Hotel Arcadia*, and of the non-fiction book *Single In The City: The Independent Woman's Handbook* and *Amitabh Bachchan*, which has just been published. She is also the co-founder of the Jhalak Prize.

The week of the referendum, I was rereading José Saramago's novel *Blindness*. If I wrote it into a story, it would be laughably crude: too heavy handed a metaphor, too obvious a connection. And besides, in fiction, who would believe it? Ludicrous!

What better metaphor for a country suddenly losing its collective sight? In Saramago's novel, a mysterious ailment robs an entire village of sight. The social order unravels rapidly with disease, hunger, poverty raging through the population and a dictatorial regime resorting to violence against the sightless citizenry.

In the year since the referendum, I have returned again and again to the book. It lies on my desk with an ever increasing number of colourful tabs to mark the passages. Every day or two, as more bad news drips out: the City relocating staff, another report detailing skyrocketing hate crime, more laughably deluded statements from politicians, I find myself picking up the book. To me it is providing better and more insightful analysis, even predictions, than all the pundits in the land.

Meanwhile, the blindness refuses to recede in Britain: one sector after another of the economy crumbles and withers away while the great and the good promise more delusions of future wealth; the leader of the opposition behaves like the doctor's wife in the novel, pretending to be blind though perhaps with more conviction and less ability to organise, help and resist; meanwhile those who have locked us all into an asylum that is rapidly deteriorating into poverty appear – like the soldiers – readying themselves to abandon us all at the worst moment. There is even some grim humour in Saramago's naming of the mysterious ailment the 'white sickness'.

One year since the referendum, I find that I am not alone in turning to literature for comfort, for understanding. For sense.

A philosopher friend with a non-British EU passport and half a century of living in England finds comfort in rereading Plato and his concept of transferred ignorance. When I meet another – a Lithuanian – friend for coffee, she is thumbing through a battered copy of Mikhail Bulgakov's *Master and Margarita*. A Spanish twice-migrant colleague repeatedly quotes – with thinly disguised panic and a great deal of laughter – the banana massacre sections from Gabriel García Márquez's *One Hundred Years of Solitude*.

While many continue to drum up hysteria about immigration and sing incessant paeans to 'taking back control' and 'sovereignty', most of my own circle, composed of immigrants of different stripes, find ourselves reduced to ciphers: we are at once taking over British jobs while also stealing benefits; we don't pay enough taxes or use up too much of the public services; we are all unwelcome or just some of us, depending on the spin of the day.

Silenced, erased, turned into nothing more than walking

targets for blame, distrust and worse, fictionalised tales of other horrors provide grim comfort: we are neither alone nor the first. Perhaps this is because many migrants are from lands where nothing can be spoken but nothing is forgotten. Far too many of us carry memories that were expunged from official records in the pores of our skins. We carry histories of oppression and resistance in our very dreams. And we know all too well that the past was never pretty baked cakes and lacy napkins and pastel buntings. That the past has always been poverty, war and horror raged by the powerful against those they label others, and, when those run out, against those they had called their own.

It is this knowledge, like an incessant itch under our skins, that keeps us safe from the affliction that has gripped Britain, for which we still have no name: malady of sightlessness; the disease of amnesia; a plague of insanity? Or perhaps it has, as viruses do, mutated into something more deadly and grotesque: a combination of all of these.

As with all grave illnesses, we keep obsessive, careful watch. Days of hope when the fever seems to recede are few and far between. We make plans and take steps, (those of us who can) finding overseas jobs, leaving our homes to find refuge elsewhere. A friend sells his house, accepting a price that is lower than he paid just a year ago. 'The prices will drop further,' he says with a shrug. He works in the City and knows his money so I believe him. Another tells me that she has sent her children to a language school in Germany for the summer. 'It's best they become fully bilingual before they have to move there.'

But what of those who cannot and will not leave? A writer

friend in her nineties who survived the Nazis tells me she dreads what comes next. She explains that she has no place to go because, after six decades of living in London, she knows no one in France. Another friend veers between stoicism ('we will endure'), defiance ('we will not be forced out') and despair ('but what if they make us leave?'). A Jewish friend – born and raised in London – tells me she has acquired Polish passports for herself and her family: 'Just in case.' I know the full horror of that choice: her parents were the only ones of her family to survive Auschwitz.

And through it all we clutch at straws, seeking anyone who may even offer the flimsiest of remedies, even voting (those of us who can) for that leader of the opposition who plays willing midwife to the ever-deepening darkness. Somewhere, somehow, perhaps like many others in the past, we hope that we will be spared. That, by some miracle, the country would decide otherwise.

On good days, we tell each other that this will pass. That we have learned from history, from horrors of the past. That it's just a blip. That it will not, cannot, get worse. On bad days, we share apocalyptic fears, joking about escape routes and countries of refuge. And around us, the country stumbles on. Blind. And blinded!

HOPE PREVAILS

Owen Jones

OWEN JONES was born in Sheffield and grew up in Stockport. After graduating, he worked as a trade union and parliamentary researcher. He is a columnist at the *Guardian* and formerly the *Independent*, and the author *of Chavs: The Demonisation of the Working Class*. His most recent book, *The Establishment: And How They Get Away With It*, was published in September 2014. He was the winner of the 2012 Stonewall Journalist of the Year and 2013 Political Book Awards Young Writer of the Year. He is now working on his third book, *The Politics of Hope*.

Arriving at ITV studios in King's Cross on referendum night, it was difficult to shake off a profound feeling of foreboding. I was utterly convinced that Britain had voted to leave the European Union. Britain seethed with discontent at the status quo, and immigration – which had been allowed, all too unchallenged, to become the prism through which so many understood their real and growing problems – dominated debate. ITV studios was where I had a spent general election night a year earlier: in the minutes before the exit poll, the faces of the Tory guests were pale, their body language defensive. Their nervousness – panic even – was ill-founded, and the atmosphere soon switched: it was like being on national television during a funeral surrounded by people having a wedding. The mood of the 2015 Conservatives was one of triumphalism. Notably, here was a sentiment the right-wing faction of the Brexiteers never had. The principal victors of the 2016 referendum were bitter winners, victors who behaved like sore losers, just like the forces of Trumpism across the Atlantic.

In the immediate term, Brexit was not – from my standpoint – a national disaster because of the economic consequences of severing Britain's relationship with the EU. Yes, it was undoubtedly the case that whatever economic pain would arrive on Britain's shores would, as ever, be suffered most by working-class people and the poorest: indeed, Leave voters among them. David Cameron and George Osborne's dire warnings of economic calamity did not materialise in the weeks after the vote, although Britain's longest squeeze in wages since the Napoleonic era did resume.

There was something far more disturbing at play. There was the hatred. The vast majority of Leave voters were not violent racists, or anything close. But every violent racist certainly woke up on 24 June 2016 with a sense of vindication and, critically, a belief they had a mandate: they cashed in with online hatred, verbal abuse or worse against minority Britons or anyone with a different accent.

For the right-wing Brexiteers, leaving the European Union was no mere readjustment of trading and constitutional arrangements. It represented something else, a cultural counter-revolution. The struggles of women, ethnic minorities and LGBTQ people for equality had yielded great conquests, all dismissed by their opponents under the umbrella term of 'political correctness'. But for the right-wing Brexiteer faction, the party was now over. You've had your fun, they now snarled, some with less subtlety than others. Dissent was recast as treason. When judges ruled that Parliament must decide when Article 50 was triggered, formally beginning Britain's negotiated exit from the EU, the *Daily Mail* denounced them as 'Enemies of the People'. When a snap election was called in order to obliterate Labour as a political force, the same newspaper demanded: 'CRUSH THE SABOTEURS!'

When I arrived at ITV studios for the third time in two

years – this time for a Tory partisan election – I had an understandable nervousness. The previous two times had not been happy experiences. Political upsets had indeed happened in the last two years, but they did not tend to favour my politics. This time proved to be different. The Tories lost their majority: and here, in a sense, was the antithesis of June 2016. The referendum result had offered frightening questions about what Britain had become. Then, in the 2017 election, 40 per cent of voters opted for a socialist-led Labour party. If 2016 was a carnival of reaction, 2017 was the defiant cry of millions who voted for a project which blamed vested elite interests, not foreigners, for the ills of society. There were many who had woken up on 24 June 2016 and wondered if they recognised their own country. June 2017 allowed them to look again and reconsider.

What the referendum result unleashed cannot be willed away. There are those among the defeated Remain side who – increasingly loudly – believe that Brexit must be overturned. The victory was only narrow, they say. When those who abstained are factored in, only a minority voted to Leave. The case of the Leave side – from money for the NHS to xenophobic hatred – was based on lies. From a legal point of view, the referendum was only advisory. The consequences of Brexit would be so disastrous for the country, it would be near criminal to allow the referendum result to be implemented.

But while the grief over the result is understandable, such arguments are more howls of rage than a strategy. If Remain had prevailed with a 52–48 per cent margin and Farage had argued that the narrowness of the result necessitated a second referendum (which he would have done), that the vote was only advisory, that the Remain vote was only 37 per cent of the electorate once non-voters were included, that the Remain campaign had lied with false claims of imminent economic armageddon – well, to suggest that Remainers would have offered short shrift is a polite understatement. It may well be that – if Brexit does indeed prove to be economically ruinous – a shift in public opinion will make a second referendum inevitable. But despite much feted anecdotes of Leave voters' buyer's remorse, the polling offers little evidence of so-called 'Bregret', and much evidence that millions of Remain voters are reconciled to a referendum result they never wanted.

Both Britain and the US have long been united by a sense of Anglo-Saxon exceptionalism. Both resisted succumbing to the irrational populist impulses of their Western counterparts, or so the narrative went. It is striking that both are now being convulsed by the most serious political crises in the Western world. Both cases are striking examples of a decaying social order. In Britain, the affordable houses people need are not built; secure and well-paid jobs are lacking; living standards have flatlined and fallen; and public services have been undermined for ideological ends. Brexit looked unthinkable to much of Britain's elite: in hindsight, perhaps what is most surprising is the narrowness of the margin of victory. Britain's social order is not just unjust, it is bankrupt and unsustainable. Its morbid symptoms are no longer possible to ignore: Brexit being perhaps the most striking example. The terms on which the referendum was won seemed to point to the triumphalist victory of right-wing populism. But Britain's future now has a far broader – and more optimistic – range of possibilities.

GOODBYE

David Shrigley

DAVID SHRIGLEY was born in 1968 and grew up in Leicester. He studied at Glasgow School of Art from 1988–91. He lived in Glasgow until 2015 and now lives in Brighton. His work encompasses many media including drawing, painting, sculpture, animation, performance and music and has been exhibited in many different countries. His drawings have appeared in numerous newspapers and magazines and he is the author of over thirty graphic books. In 2012 he had a retrospective exhibition at Hayward Gallery in London, he was shortlisted for the Turner Prize in 2013 and he was awarded the 2016 Fourth Plinth commission for Trafalgar Square.

GOOD
BYE

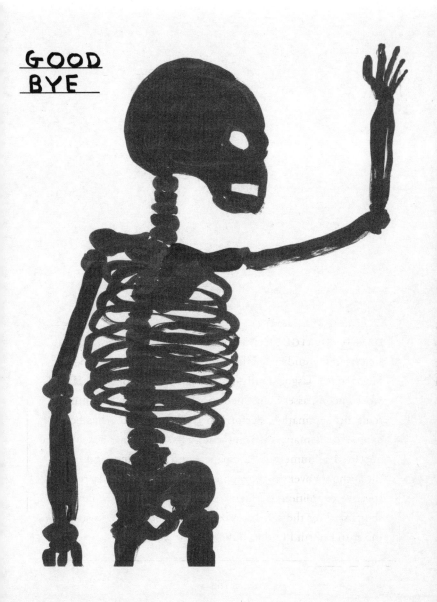

RIGHT AND WRONG

Ben Collins

BEN COLLINS, formerly 'The Stig' from BBC's *Top Gear*, has crossed Europe's borders faster than any human. He imported a truffle from Italy aboard a Bugatti Veyron at 250 mph, slammed James Bond's Aston Martin around Lake Garda in *Quantum of Solace* and was the fastest driver to lap Le Mans during a monsoon. A Champion racing driver and world-renowned Hollywood stunt driver, Ben has written two bestselling books: *The Man in the White Suit*, his high-octane autobiography, and *How to Drive,* his indispensable guide to life's essential driving skills, along with a few stunt tips and survival secrets.

The Lear jet banked and swung into Warsaw's southern airstrip. I steadied my Earl Grey as the wheels kissed the tarmac and scanned through the porthole for a glimpse of the production team for my new TV show, *Automaniak*. A massive limousine and a security detail spotlit by halogen lamps; it had to be them.

I strode down the jetway. A Polish version of Rob Lowe, in a Mafioso suit and sunglasses, presumed to take my suitcase. He had a kind face. I cuffed it with an open-handed slap, and walked towards the camera to complete the shot and meet the producer.

Tears were rolling off the producer's cheeks. The cameraman was also convulsed with laughter, which meant the lens was too. Punching Patryk, Poland's leading car show host, wasn't in the official script, so we filmed my 'big arrival' again to fool the Polish audience into believing I was a nice guy.

I had actually landed the day before on a low budget knee-crusher. The words 'No Schengen' were daubed across the border in lettering large enough for the most myopic traveller to read them from Mars. Ironic, given Poland's accession to the EU's free movement area. After passing muster with the border guards, I finally reached my contact on his phone. He

BEN COLLINS

explained that they were drunk and would not be collecting me from the airport.

Eventually, Patryk scooped me up personally and took us to the hotel, inaptly named The Glamour, where my new boss was wedged to the ceiling by a ten-foot-high gate preventing access to the foyer. We pulled his flailing limbs while those on the other side pushed, to aid his desperate mission to obtain more whisky.

I bonded surprisingly quickly with my new friends and learned that while vodka has its place in Poland, especially when consuming raw meat, whisky and 7Up was the party fuel. It didn't take me long to recognise that discretion on this occasion was the better part of valour, so I moved for a loo break, with every intention of diverting directly to bed.

'Good, you are sensible, Ben,' applauded the director. 'Goodnight.'

He explained that all Poles knew the 'British Goodbye', the backdoor boogie with which we excuse ourselves from a party while the going is good, before everyone starts dancing like dying insects. But you remain friends in the morning.

The EU is still in the whisky faze. Debt-fuelled and democratically bankrupt, with the totalitarian fantasy of forcing the wonderfully heterogeneous peoples of Europe to march to the same impossible tune. No, I won't miss the hubris of not-elected-by-you commission officials creating tone-deaf statutes and ways to enforce them. Thankfully 'the EU' is merely an institution, totally removed from the inhabitants of Europe to whom I won't be saying goodbye at all.

'England is in effect insular, she is maritime, she is linked through her interactions, her markets, her supply lines to the most diverse and often the most distant countries . . .' No, not Churchill, but French President De Gaulle after blocking the UK from joining the EU – then, the EEC – for the second time. De Gaulle was right. We are a global-minded people, rather than belonging to a closed clique.

As HMS *Queen Elizabeth* sailed off to her new role with NATO (the only organisation that actually protects Europe) it dawned on me that Britain has twice as many aircraft carriers as Russia, and twice her GDP. And have you ever noticed that – or wondered why – all carriers, even Chinese and American, have their control towers on the right-hand side of their landing decks? It's so that the only obstacle pilots might accidentally crash into is in their dominant field of vision.

A few thousand years ago the clever Romans dug mines and quarries across Britain, and archaeologists were able to discern from the grooves worn by horse and cart that they drove on the left side of the road. Their network stretched from the Appian Way to trunk roads like the A5 which still connect Britain.

They didn't do much by accident, the Romans. The majority of us are right-handed and right-eye dominant. Passing road users coming in the other direction from this optimal position afforded a stronger view of traffic, and freed a sword arm to cut off any road rage. The entire world followed this logic, until the French got involved.

Napoleon was both short and left-handed. He made his armies march on the right-hand side of the road and enforced the practice throughout the countries he conquered. The Duke of Wellington's armies prevented the madness from infecting Britain and her colonies, but the rot was setting in.

The Americans began using French style pack-horse teams to haul goods and went along with driving on the wrong side of the highway. Along with pouring tea into Boston Harbor, it was their way to celebrate the freedom to legislate independently of the old empire. Once Henry Ford and co. mass-produced their cars with steering wheels on the left, other countries imported them and tended to follow suit.

Adolf Hitler's insistence that Germany's jet-powered Messerschmitts be used as bombers rather than fighters was one of many decisions that cost him the war, and saved our bomber crews from being savaged by high-speed predators. He also extended right-hand-side driving to the parts of Europe that Napoleon failed to reach.

So today, two-thirds of the world's population use their weaker eye to clock oncoming traffic and overtake, all because of an undersized Frenchman and an argument about some tea leaves. Britain, India, Australia and Japan remain notable exceptions to the decline in common sense, like all civilised tea-drinking nations should.

But I'm not done with French bureaucracy just yet.

In Britain we give way to the right, and thereby avoid accidents at every junction by applying a device called the brake. So our cousins across *La Manche* must give way to the left? *Non. La priorité à droite* means that traffic on a main road has to give way to any lunatic entering, unseen, from a side road. So you can drive towards a French roundabout at full speed, and those already on it must yield or die. *Ce n'est pas magnifique. C'est la guerre!*

France would love to change this archaic, deluded system

– but it's enshrined in statute, so it can only be changed by a government ruling, which takes decades.

Brits can take credit for a number of innovations over the years: nuclear fission, TV, the telephone, radar, the internet, to name but a few. Oh, and hand-wringing. But long before pessimism became the national sport, we also developed a unique system of common law; the envy of the modern world.

Unlike the sluggish statutory legal system, the raison d'être of the EU, common law evolves case by case, through debate and court judgements on principles of equity, like a hungry animal. It embraces trends and doesn't require prolonged government regulation to turn Sense into Law. Our corporate governance is second to none, and most English-speaking nations would agree, America included. It's *because* we don't have a written constitution, rather than despite it, that we can adapt swiftly to the future.

And Moore's Law, not EU law, will be forging that future.

Moore's Law – that computers double their processing power every two years – has led to a forecast that half of existing jobs will be performed by automatons in 2030, and driving will be among the first to go. Despite my passion for rights of passage, I'm going to sit back and enjoy the ride while Robbie Robot whisks me – where?

Across the Loire Valley, of course, to pick up a bag of oysters and a fine bottle of Muscadet, and then on to the greatest race on Earth: Le Mans.

A bientôt, mes amis.

FRENCH LESSONS

Henry Marsh

HENRY MARSH originally read PPE at Oxford University before – as he puts it – straying into brain surgery. Shortly before retiring from the NHS he published *Do No Harm*, a memoir of his life as a neurosurgeon. This received rapturous reviews, went on to become an international bestseller, and was translated into thirty languages. He subsequently published *Admissions*, a *Sunday Times* number one bestseller, which describes the aftermath of his leaving the NHS and his continuing work abroad in countries as diverse as Ukraine and Nepal.

Between the ages of six and eight I lived in Scheveningen, the fishing port for The Hague, in the Netherlands, as my father had taken a two-year sabbatical from his Oxford college to head up a recently founded international legal organisation. Its purpose was to strengthen the rule of law in the post-war and post-colonial world. He was rather put out when he learned, many years later, that the initial funding for the organisation came, covertly, from the CIA. I did not learn any Dutch because I was sent to an English school. It was in a two-storey building – the ground floor was the English school and the upper floor a French school. The French children would sometimes enjoy themselves leaning over the bannisters of the staircase and spitting on us.

On our return to England I was sent to a famous prep school where the most junior French classes were taught by a certain Mr Dodds, an elderly man with rather long white hair. I have vague memories of having to stand up and recite the declination of French verbs, and having to climb into the large wooden wastepaper basket in the corner of the room if I made mistakes. The classroom wall had a large black and white lithograph entitled 'British Cavalry Clearing Out a German Machine Gun Nest', showing a successful attack – an event, I was to appreciate later, that was deeply implausible. There were two large gold and blue volumes at home, which I think my father had had as a child, called *Our Island Story* and *Our Empire Story* and I enjoyed reading the racist and jingoist adventure stories with happy innocence.

Nevertheless, for reasons I cannot readily explain, I was always very proud of the fact that my mother was German. She was a political refugee who escaped from Germany in 1939, just before the war started. In the school playground between lessons the other boys would rush about with outstretched arms claiming to be Spitfires, but I was a Messerschmitt. Inconsistently, however, I was very upset when one boy took to calling me Jerrybags. Why the suffix 'bags' was an insult I do not know. Perhaps it was something to do with debagging – the occasional assault and removal of the trousers of an unpopular boy. This particular boy's father ran the main dairy shop in the town and my wise and clever elder sister, when I told her of my distress, suggested I riposte with Milkbags – which worked very well.

The teaching of French at my next school was little better and my deep fear and loathing of the language was confirmed by the occasional family holiday in France, where the French would greet my attempts to communicate in their language with expressions of pain and disgust. I had the choice of doing Greek, German or Geography for O level and although I was keen to learn German, my father – despite being a convinced internationalist who spoke good German and French – insisted that I study ancient Greek. This is just about the only resentment I have against him.

When we are young we have a wonderful facility for learning

languages. The neuroscientific basis of this is not known, but it presumably is connected to the way that children's brains have an extraordinary ability to make new synapses, the electro-chemical links between the 80 billion nerve cells in our brains. Up to the age of two, children can discriminate between all the different possible phonemes but then their brains start to become hard-wired, at least for sound. Chinese children, for instance, lose the ability to discriminate between 'r' and 'l' – between rice and lice.

I lost the miraculous ability to learn foreign languages many years ago. I am deeply ashamed that I am, effectively, monolingual, unlike the rest of my family. I refused to take part in any foreign student exchanges and associated Europe with anxiety and feelings of loss of control. And yet this ti-midity on my part engendered in me a feeling of inferiority about being English rather than of defensive superiority, and I longed to have closer contact with the European mainland. Perhaps in some way I was hoping to reassert my German heritage. This eventually took the form of spending my spare time away from medical work in England, working pro bono in Ukraine. I liked to think that I was helping that troubled watershed of a country to move towards the freedom and the rule of law which we enjoy in Western Europe, away from the Soviet past and the cynical authoritarianism of Russia in the East. For my friends and colleagues in Ukraine, Europe is the promised land and they are desperate to be part of it and to be seen to be part of it. This has made Brexit all the more painful for me.

I remember when I was studying PPE at Oxford in the late 1960s, how I had to write essays on the weakness of the British economy – the so-called 'sick man of Europe'. You can never predict the future, and the economic future of Britain will depend as much on the world economy as on the particular details of any Brexit deal, but I am puzzled by the way that the proponents of Brexit seem to have forgotten the recent past. They seem to think that somehow the country will return to the triumphant past – to the nineteenth century when Britain dominated the world economy (but also conducted the Opium Wars), or even, more absurdly, to the swash-buckling age of Elizabeth I and Shakespeare. But the EU for me was never about economics – for all its flaws, it was about law and freedom and deliberation and inclusiveness, even if it was so often boring and bureaucratic and moved with the speed of a snail. Instead, with Brexit, we may well get to live in a new age – but a mean and petty one, overseen by leaders with all the intellectual rigour of a tabloid headline.

BORDERS

Alex Kapranos

ALEX KAPRANOS is the lead singer and guitarist for the band Franz Ferdinand. He is the author of *Sound Bites*. He lives somewhere in Scotland.

Borders. I don't think about borders. I arrive, queue, place my electronic passport on the scanner, the glass doors slide apart. I move on. I don't think.

It was February 2001 when Charlie and Ally asked if I'd go with them to Kosovo. Ally's stepdad was a trucker. He drove backline for The Who and Led Zep in the 1970s, but was now a blacksmith in the Highlands, who still occasionally drove for an NGO called HALO that removes mines after conflict. They were in Kosovo, clearing up after Milošević, but had lost funding, or maybe the permission to be there. I can't remember exactly why, but they could no longer stay, even though there were still mines to pull from the ground. Now they had to get their gear back. He was going to drive a road train of two articulated trailers pulled by one cab, but needed volunteers to drive a convoy of ambulances. That's when I was called. It seemed a good idea. Go to Kosovo. Drive an ambulance back to Scotland. I asked my boss if I could get four days off work. Sure thing. It seemed like a good idea.

We met at Glasgow Airport and were joined by my friend Tom and another ten or so drivers, making up an odd mismatch of a group united by a relative lack of responsibility. Half of us were either unemployed or in crappy jobs where we were dispensable and the rest were recently retired. The plan was to fly to Pristina, drive across to Bar in Montenegro, get the ferry to Bari in Italy then drive back to Dumfriesshire, where HALO is based.

It was dark when we landed at the military airport. The absence of streetlamps or noticeable road markings made the journey to the camp disorienting. When we got there we found a compound with high walls, razor wire and lookout towers. We were met by a couple of guys in their early thirties, ex-military, friendly and tough. Tough in a way I don't properly understand. I'm not tough. These guys looked like they could run for a long time and not moan about it. Or get shot and not moan too much either. I'm not tough. I moan if I have to exert myself to the point of engaging my Ventolin inhaler. The other drivers were not tough either: maybe slightly tougher than me, but not much. I saw wariness and flickering insecurity in their eyes, and wondered how much they could see in mine. They disguised it with stories. Blokey stories. Stories about women and boozing and capacity for blokey behaviour. Whisky appeared and was drunk.

The morning smelled of dead smoke and the view was of a grey mud field where the edges disappeared into heavy mist. One of the drivers had knocked something over and part of the camp had briefly caught fire during the night, leaving the smell, but not too much damage. The vehicles were in the yard. A huge digger with wheels taller than me was strapped to the first trailer. The wheels were covered in chainmail with links as thick as a thigh. The other trailer carried a shipping container rammed with equipment. The ambulances were parked beside them.

The ambulances were part of the HALO working day. No matter how painstaking and diligent they were when clearing, a mine would occasionally go off, taking part of a volunteer leg, so the ambulance would be there, always waiting. These had been donated by the Dutch army and were Land Rovers. Not the modern luxury Land Rovers that well-paid footballers drive, but raw machinery from 1966 with an oversized cabin welded on the back with enough space for two stretchers. An old-fashioned blue light perched on top and a green cross painted on the side. Don't take it over thirty miles an hour, not that there will be an opportunity to until Italy anyway. Don't use the brakes going down the mountains. They can't handle it and will burn up. Use the gears instead. Don't overtake. Stay in the cab. There's no heater. Wear all your clothes.

The complete destruction of infrastructure strikes you first. There is no refuse collection. Polythene bags and rubbish are scattered everywhere. Shops do not exist, so there is no advertising. What can you advertise when there is nothing to sell? Hoardings still stand by the road, but are blank, ripped paper and have been for years. Trade consists of guys with trestle tables on the roadside selling contraband, mainly cigarettes. Then you notice the graves. Fresh graves. Graves with flimsy wooden markers. Sometimes a photograph. Clusters of graves. Families of graves.

We drove to a river where the surface of the earth had been scraped raw. No field, road, tree or permanent man-made feature, only raw red earth with a river running across it. Maybe there was a bridge once. We drove through the river. There were no cars, only UN pickups and trucks. We kept driving. The cab was noisy and diesel fumes came through a hole in the floor. My hands were cold inside my gloves on the Bakelite steering wheel. The sensation of being alone but part of the slow convoy of smoking ambulances following the articulated road train was exhilarating.

The ascent started into the Prokletije Mountains. Accursed Mountains: that's what it translates as, or the Albanian Alps if you're avoiding the drama. They were imposing, monochrome and darkening. It was dusk when we reached the Kosovo/UN border, a cursory checkpoint, then into no man's land. The Montenegrin border was another hour's drive, but until then it was a demilitarised zone of disputed territory, not Kosovo, not Montenegro, no government, no law, no road surface. The weak headlights of the Land Rover would dimly light scenes of furtive unloading of trucks, abandoned trailers, cigarettes. Cartons and cartons of cigarettes. The gears ground and the engine whined. We continued. Ears popped. The snow stacked in blackened walls lining the road, dense pine muffling the sound beyond. The snow became everything, the road, the windscreen, the air.

All of the vehicles stopped. We were by the border, but were going to wait until morning to cross. To conserve heat, we doubled up, two to the back of each ambulance. Tom joined me in mine, a stretcher each. The metal poles of the stretcher were slightly narrower than the width of my shoulders as I lay on the rough canvas suspended between them. I was inside four sleeping bags, wore an oversized puffa and all my socks, and was still cold. We lay there laughing at how cold we were, chatting about Glasgow and bands by the light of a torch. An ancient rusty trail ran across the roof in a dry splatter, shot from an artery by someone lying on this stretcher. I was guessing, imagining the scene. How else would it have got there? Only an artery would have the strength to get that range. I asked Tom what he thought and he was asleep.

Morning was bright, snow reflections of feeble warmth and light. I jumped out the back of the ambulance and looked at the absurd beauty of where we were. I could see a set of log buildings further down the hill and dark shapes cut into the snow. There was activity. Some of the Land Rovers were stuck in the snow. Those that weren't used their winches to drag them back onto the harder compressed snow of the road. We lined up, back in convoy, ready to move to the crossing. This time there was going to be bureaucracy, but we were prepared. Paperwork, three times, explained who we were and why we were there. Among the papers were the envelopes. In the envelopes was the cash. Crossing the border required the payment of admin fees to the officials. Fine, we were all ready, knew the situation, so the convoy coughed into motion, crawling down the road to the crossing, the truck first and, for no particular reason, my ambulance last.

We pulled up in front of the log huts and got out of our cabs with the paperwork. I looked to my left among the trees at the dark shapes I'd seen cut out of the snow and realised they were slits that had been cut into snow-covered bivouacs or shelters. Behind the slits were machine guns pointing at us. We walked into the huts and queued.

A bench was partitioned into three sections, a dour soldier behind each one. The process was as mundane as paying a gas bill, as tedious as signing on. We waited, each driver took their turn to present their paperwork, have it looked over, stamped, signed, carbon copies ripped, passport scrutinised, then on to the next admin soldier to repeat every detail. Eventually it was my turn. There were guns and accursed mountains outside, but it was reaching church sermon levels of boredom as I stood there and the first guy went through every line on every sheet. Thorough thorough thorough. I moved on to the next admin soldier. He began to repeat what the first guy had done. Carbon copies, signatures, passport, stamps, ink, envelope, thorough, thorough, thorough. Time was treacle rolling down a slight incline, barely perceptible in its movement. Charlie completed in front of me, left the hut, I was passed my papers and moved on to the last admin soldier guy. I was last in the room and passed over the last of the papers, passport, envelope, rustling, stamp, stamp, scribbled officious signing, thorough thorough, thorough. A barking of something in Serbo-Croat, an examination of the passport again. Another Serbo-Croat exclamation and this time I realised he was expecting to hear an answer.

This was unexpected. This hadn't happened to the others. I don't speak Serbo . . . was I thinking it or saying it? I looked up. He was pointing at my passport. Pointing at me. He was animated and formal simultaneously. He said something again. I'm sorry, I don't . . . No smile. Another exclamation and a jabbing of the finger at my photograph, at my face, and he disappeared behind a door with the passport.

My head thumped a little with the situation. What was his problem with the passport? Was he going to come back with it? Did he need another envelope? I didn't have any more cash on me. Was it because of my name? No, it seemed to be the photograph. Shit, it was my hair. Or something. It was different. The photograph was old. I had the black quiff and big stupid sideburns. Maybe he thought it wasn't me. Was he speaking to me in Serbo-Croat like the officer in *The Great Escape* when he wishes Gordon Jackson 'good luck' in English to catch him out? But I'm not escaping. I'm just crossing the border. Bollocks, everyone else was already through. I wondered how far down the road they'd get before they noticed I hadn't. Churning, churning thoughts.

I stared into middle-space and the soldier returned without me looking up. He had more paperwork now and was laying it on the bench, jabbing at it with the finger, jabbing at the passport. I wasn't looking at it, but sort of through it, it was there, but there was no focus. He was talking a lot. Waving the paperwork at me. I focused and it was different. More pointing. It looked different from the other paperwork. It was a magazine. A pornographic magazine. He was pointing at the passport, at the photograph. He was pointing at me. He was pointing at me and sort of laughing. Was that a laugh? I wasn't sure. He was pointing at the guy in the magazine. He was pointing the passport. I began laughing. Oh yeah. Look. That guy. Yeah, he does look a bit like … Yeah, ha ha. There are three of them. Man, that's filthy. Ha ha. Yeah. Look. Look at the picture. He was still laughing and passed my paperwork back.

Charlie was waiting outside the door.

Everything OK? What's so funny?

I don't think about borders. I scan my electronic passport and move on. Except sometimes. Sometimes I think of that border when I cross these easy borders.

WHAT WE TALK
ABOUT WHEN WE
TALK ABOUT POIROT

Val McDermid

VAL McDERMID grew up in Fife. Edinburgh was her first city and most of the world has been a disappointment since. Val has been dubbed the Queen of Crime and her thirty-one novels have been translated into over forty languages and have sold more than 15 million copies worldwide. Among the many awards on her mantelpiece are the Gold Dagger, the Diamond Dagger, the *LA Times* Book of the Year Award, the Theakston's Old Peculier Book of the Year and Outstanding Contribution to Crime Fiction awards, the Grand Prix des Romans d'Aventure and the Lambda Literary Foundation Pioneer Award. Her series featuring psychological profiler Tony Hill and police officer Carol Jordan was adapted for the award-winning TV series *Wire in the Blood*, which has been shown in over forty countries. There's probably a repeat showing somewhere right now . . .

Val is also a regular broadcaster on BBC radio and TV, as a commentator, as a documentary writer and presenter, and as a radio dramatist. A keen quizzer, Val represents Scotland in BBC Radio4's *Round Britain Quiz*. She's also appeared successfully on several TV quizzes including *Celebrity Mastermind*, *Only Connect*, *Pointless* and *Eggheads*. In the Christmas alumni University Challenge series, she captained the St Hilda's College, Oxford, team to victory – the first ever all-woman team to take the crown.

Her latest venture is as the singer in a rock and roll band – Fun Lovin' Crime Writers. Val and fellow writers Stuart Neville, Doug Johnstone, Mark Billingham and Luca Veste perform cover versions of an array of songs, most of which feature murder. Their debut wowed the Edinburgh International Book Festival in 2017 and next year they'll be murdering more songs for fun.

In case you think this is all too much fun, she's also a director of Raith Rovers Football Club, which keeps her feet firmly planted on the ground.

When I first began publishing crime fiction thirty years ago, the place we looked to for challenging approaches to the genre was the US. Writers such as Sara Paretsky and James Ellroy were breaking new ground, challenging us to consider fresh narrative possibilities. But crucially, there wasn't much option if we wanted to explore beyond the relatively narrow confines of British detective stories. Whatever was going on in the non-Anglophone world was a different kind of mystery. Back then, the UK publishing industry seemed almost allergic to translated fiction.

There were a few isolated exceptions. Some of Georges Simenon's Maigret stories were in print, and the innovative police procedurals of the Swedish partnership of Sjöwall and Wahlöö had been published in hardback. But our world view was shaped by an English-speaking culture, and not just in the crime genre.

Thankfully that's one aspect of publishing in general, and crime fiction in particular, that has changed dramatically in those intervening years. Some might argue that our membership of the EU has had nothing to do with that change; I would disagree profoundly.

There's no doubt that the single market has made publishing

across borders much easier. Contractually and practically, it's been more straightforward to negotiate rights for translation and foreign publication.

But far more important, I believe, is the cultural impact. Fiction is one of the ways we understand the world; it extends our horizons and awareness of the ways other people think and feel. It helps us to grasp the commonalities as much as the differences between ourselves and others. We gain an insight into histories and circumstances we've no direct personal experience of, and that understanding breeds acceptance, compassion and tolerance.

As we grew closer to our fellow European citizens, so did our appetite for understanding what we'd embarked upon, I believe. Publishers – ever quick to spot a business opportunity – realised that our increasing curiosity might provoke us into widening the compass of our reading.

For years, we writers had been insisting that, really, it made more sense to publish a cracking Swedish or French novel rather than another mediocre English one. My own calendar included festivals and book tours in Europe where I was constantly embarrassed at not having been able to read the work of colleagues who were clearly respected, admired and loved by their audiences.

Like water dripping on stone, it eventually had an impact. It started with a handful of Nordic writers and gathered momentum. Peter Høeg's *Miss Smilla's Feeling for Snow* was a hit, creating an appetite for more windows into that world. We recognised enough about those societies, the way they were organised and their shared values, to feel comfortable. We grasped the meaning of what we were reading; we saw some of the concerns of our own social democracy reflected in these stories. Karin Fossum, Henning Mankell and Arnaldur Indriðason became regulars in our bookshops and libraries.

Then the global phenomenon of Stieg Larsson's Millennium Trilogy galvanised readers and publishers both. It was like Schengen for books. The walls came down and we could finally go where we wanted. Sicily with Andrea Camilleri. Barcelona with Manuel Vázquez Montalbán. Paris with Fred Vargas. Stockholm with Arne Dahl. Berlin with Jakob Arjouni.

I admit, I relished the insight this provided into the lives of our European neighbours. Through the medium of crime fiction, I learned the reasons why the custom of the country is as it is. I found threads of their social fabric that helped me make sense of our own. The more I've read about European elsewheres, the more European I've come to feel. And conversely, as America has grown more fractured, insular and sectarian, the less I've felt comfortable there. Now, when I visit America, it just makes me feel more determinedly European.

On a more frivolous level, the new wave of European crime fiction has fulfilled another function. Forget tedious travel guides with their top ten sights. More often than not, crime novels have a powerful sense of place. What better way to get the flavour of our holiday destination than to snuggle down under the covers with a detective for our guide? We don't have to rely on translated fiction either. We can turn to the expertise of English-speaking authors who settled in Europe and provide us with their take on their adopted homes. Donna Leon's Venice, Robert Wilson's Seville and Peter May's Paris are object lessons in showing us the connective tissue between them and us.

And it cuts both ways. As Europeans have come to live among us in significant numbers, British crime writers have turned their gaze on them. Eva Dolan, Anya Lipska and Nicci French, among others, have chosen to place those immigrants at the heart of their work. And that illuminates us as well as them.

I'll leave the economic and political arguments about Brexit to others better qualified to quantify its impact. The disasters I feel impending in those areas will be on us soon enough, the macro and the micro.

What I'm most exercised about right now is being ripped apart from what I've come to feel is part of the fabric of my identity. I'm not just Scottish, not just British, but European. I feel kinship with Italians, with Germans, with Greeks. And I like that feeling. Their countries have inspired my work. I've set bits of books all over Europe – Spain, Germany, Holland, Croatia, Greece, Italy.

And now that's going to be irredeemably fragmented. In one of his more inane soundbites, Boris Johnson said we were leaving the European Union, not Europe. But already the contempt and derision have started. Just the other week in Charles de Gaulle airport, my partner mildly rebuked a young man for pushing into a queue for passport inspection. 'You are British,' he sneered, flicking his fingers in a contemptuous gesture. 'In two years, you will have no right to be here.'

My first reaction to the Brexit vote was incomprehension, followed almost immediately by rage. How could the other 52 per cent have thought for a nanosecond that it made sense to choose isolationism over collaboration? The EU is far from perfect, but walking away now is like turning your back on your family because your grandfather always gets the best of the pork crackling on the Sunday joint. You don't make things better by climbing into a bunker and pulling the lid shut.

But now the first shock has passed, my rage has metamorphosed. What I'm feeling now is grief. I'm grieving at the hard-won affinities that are coming under threat, the bonds that look likely to be severed, the understanding that will buckle and bend into something deeply unpleasant.

After the Scottish independence referendum, when I was on the losing side, I was moved to tears. But I didn't feel anger and contempt for those who voted 'No'. It didn't fracture friendships, it didn't stop me respecting their informed choice. I don't feel like that about Brexit. Part of my grief is the burn of blame. I want to shout, 'How could you? How could you be so short-sighted? How could you do this to us?'

Call me simplistic, but I wish they'd all been force-fed a diet of European crime fiction. If they'd understood nothing else, they might have grasped the underlying concept – bad things happen to people who do bad things.

SPECIAL

Cathy Rentzenbrink

CATHY RENTZENBRINK is the author of *The Last Act of Love* and *A Manual for Heartache*. Cathy speaks and writes regularly on literacy, literature and everything in between and is happiest when talking to strangers about books. She won the Snaith and District Ladies Darts Championship when she was seventeen but is now sadly out of practice.

I've never understood the urge to boast of superior British values. Is it part of a refusal to confront the murkier aspects of our past? Or simply a need to be special?

I am the daughter of a grateful immigrant. My Irish father took his first steps on English soil in 1965. He was a fifteen-year-old deck boy working on a ship transporting containers between Dublin and Liverpool. Three years later he sailed into Falmouth and met my mother on Custom House Quay. No one expected their romance to last but they are still together and still in love and my dad has never regretted making England his home. In his younger days, he was often arrested for being Irish in the wrong place at the wrong time but this never dented his gratitude to the country that has given him a family, a livelihood and plenty of food. 'I was always hungry in Ireland,' he'll say, 'and then I came to England and was never hungry again.' There was also the question of religion. Having suffered at the hands of the Christian Brothers, he valued living in a society not in thrall to the priests. My dad's voice is the soundtrack to my childhood. He would sing of brave republican heroes badly treated by the British but really he just wants everyone to get along and be left in peace to look after their families. When my brother and I went on a school trip to London when the IRA were still active on the mainland, he said, 'If anything happens to you I'll go over to Derry and strangle that bastard Gerry Adams with my own hands.'

My husband, Erwyn, was born in Edam in the Netherlands, a historic city noted mainly for its round red cheeses. His journey to England started when he got a job at the Waterstones in Amsterdam. He loved the work and when an opportunity came up at the big shop in Piccadilly he moved to England. It was 2000. We met in 2004 at the induction day for a new flagship on Oxford Street. Five years later we had a son and called him Matthew Jan. We didn't bother about getting him a Dutch passport, we're all Europeans, we thought.

Erwyn didn't get a vote in the referendum that would see him rebranded as an EU national, variously an object of suspicion, a bargaining chip or a problem to be solved. We stumbled through that Friday, the day after the referendum, trying to grasp what had happened. We watched Nigel Farage on telly, claiming a victory while flanked by flag-waving men with pasty white faces. We went to Matt's school show, to see him and his seven-year-old classmates perform a festival of the world. I cried as I watched the topknots and headscarves jostle in among the blond and ginger heads. Matt's school is the sort of multicultural dream that gives Ukippers nightmares. His best friends are from South Africa, Bangladesh, Israel, America and Wales.

Most of the people I know in London are like me, like us. We are hotchpotches, mongrels, we've been stirred in a melting pot. Everyone is half this, or a quarter that, or just arrived from somewhere else altogether. It's a sign of the times, surely. My maternal grandparents grew up within twenty miles of each other and met at the Odeon in Falmouth where he was a projectionist and she was an usherette. They hardly left Cornwall and didn't have passports, but their grandchildren all have Irish or Polish blood and their great-grandchildren are also Dutch, Ghanaian or Turkish. There's not an English surname among us. I assume other families are like this. I'm always shocked to be reminded that not everyone is moved by the hope that difference might be something to celebrate rather than to fear.

Matt came home recently and asked me why Trump doesn't like brown people. Another day he asked if there was going to be World War Three. And another: 'Mummy, if you die, will Daddy and I have to go and live in Holland?'

'No, darling, of course not,' I said, not knowing if I was telling the truth. What are they going to do to my husband if they can't cash in the bargaining chip in the way they want? Send him home? What happens to us? Part of me thinks that is melodramatic catastrophising, yet I didn't see Brexit coming. I don't trust my own instincts any more, I no longer trust in my idea of what my country is.

Discussing all this with a friend, he said, 'Sorry, I always forget that Brexit has a personal dimension for you. I don't think of Erwyn as being foreign.'

Nor do I, somehow. Erwyn's English is flawless. No one clocks him as a foreigner by his accent. It only comes out in conversation about where his name comes from or which football team he supports. When we go to Holland now, everyone there laughs at his accent and replies to him in English. He's never wanted residency or to be a UK citizen. He wanted what he had, to be a Dutch person but to live and work here and think of himself as settled. If Erwyn was single, he'd leave, he tells me. He doesn't want to live where he isn't wanted. But it's not as simple as that. Like no doubt many other EU nationals, he is knitted into the fabric of UK society. He has a wife and a son, and our life is here. We're muddling on.

My dad, too, sounds almost more English than Irish these days, though he retains a pleasing lilt. He's lived here happily for fifty years. A lot of his gratitude had rubbed off on me. I quite liked my country. Not with the flag waving zeal of a Little Englander still having wet dreams over our colonial past, but in a world full of injustice I thought this was a good place to live. I hoped things were getting better and fairer. Now Brexit has revealed the extent of my naivety. If we'd wanted to invent something to shine a light on our grubby institutions, our greedy, self-serving politicians and our easily duped electorate we couldn't have found anything better. We've allowed our wrong-headed delusions of grandeur to lead us to a terrible place. This conviction that we are special, that we would be better and greater alone, has amplified our divisions in a move that feels the exact opposite of truth and reconciliation. Lies and destruction, more like, leading to an act of colossal self-harm. It's at best pointless and expensive, at worst, well, I don't like to think about it. I do wonder whether we'll look back and see that part of the problem was that we'd become complacent. We lost the plot on what the point of Europe was. We talked about trade deals when we should have been thinking about preserving peace.

What can I do about it? I don't know. I have never felt more like chaining myself to railings or throwing stones at the windows of those in power but I'm not sure to what end. I don't want to succumb to anger and hatred. Or insanity. The longer I look at Brexit the madder it seems and the madder I feel. When Theresa May talks about superior British values I boil with rage. Why do we want to be better than other people? Why would we not want to be global citizens? How have we allowed a minority of racists and xenophobes to bring us to this? It feels like a coup. I don't recognise my country. I'm full of shame every time one of our politicians crosses the English Channel. To borrow one of my dad's favourite expressions: what a shower of shits they are.

To stay sane I've had to stop watching and reading the news. I largely have to keep off Twitter because it makes me want to scream obscenities in all directions. I dream that I do this, that I get stuck in a loop of tweeting Fuckoffyoucunt at various politicians and commentators. Another night I dreamed I was God. I was fed up of having to listen to Theresa May's prayers, but even as God I didn't have any power to do anything except put my head in my hands.

The optimistic, grateful part of me still hopes that sanity will reassert itself, that people will think, hang on a second, now that we understand the scale of the job, it doesn't seem like such a good idea after all. Maybe other things, not least peace across the Irish Sea, are more important than this mirage of taking back control.

Whatever happens with Brexit, I'll always be a European by birth, by marriage and by inclination. I've been thinking of Voltaire a lot lately as I cultivate my garden. It does feel like small act of rebellion. I won't be incapacitated by impotent fury. I refuse to spend my time in anguished staring at screens when I could be hanging out with my son enjoying his innate sense of justice and doing my bit in helping him become a good human. I hum Whitney Houston. I have to believe that the children are our future. 'You're special,' I say to my half-Dutch, quarter-Irish son, 'And so is everybody else.'

BANANAS AND DILDOS

Matt Frei

MATT (MATTHIAS) FREI was born in the German steel city of Essen before moving to the gambling mecca of Baden Baden, and, at the age of eight, to London. He has lived in Jerusalem, Berlin, Rome, Hong Kong and Singapore, covered the Balkan Wars as the BBC's southern Europe correspondent, the fall of the Suharto regime as the BBC's Asia correspondent, and the rise and fall of President Bush as Washington correspondent. He has interviewed five American presidents, including Donald Trump, and presented the Emmy and Peabody Award-winning BBC World News America. He moved to Channel Four News as Washington correspondent and then presenter and Europe editor, where he became RTS TV Journalist of the Year in 2015 and 2017. He is married with four children, and remains a proud citizen of nowhere.

My mother had warned me they would come. 'They know where to find you. They're a bit afraid. They have no idea what to make of it all. Although I suspect they are much more interested in seeing the inside of your hotel.' She was calling from Bonn, and signed off in her usual curt fashion.

I looked around my room. The absurdly gothic four-poster bed. The twirled black phone receiver that had been strapped to the wall with grey gaffer tape for the permanently open line to London. The pneumatically fluffed pillows. The oversized chandelier.

I was enveloped inside a huge white dressing gown embossed with the hotel's crescent and GRAND HOTEL UNTER DEN LINDEN. I was about to turn twenty-six, and as a veteran colleague from the *New York Times* had told me over the horizon of his distended belly in the sauna the day before: 'This is the best story you will ever cover, and you've only just started. You poor son of a bitch!'

I had wondered whether he was talking about the swanky hotel or the news, which everyone agreed deserved to be called 'Historic'.

It was early November, and the throat-scratching fog – hints of coal dust mingled with cheap diesel and cabbage – had descended on East Berlin. Visibility had been reduced to fifty metres. The world was transfixed by events in the divided city. But the revolution was confined to a grey Tupperware box. The muffled voices, delivered in East Germany's strangulated Saxon accent, were an echo chamber of disbelief.

The mood had been changing ever since tens of thousands of East Germans had simply refused to come back from their package holidays in Hungary or Czechoslovakia.

First, they were given passage on trains to the West. Then the demonstrations started in Leipzig. Every week, another layer of fear was discarded. The striptease of freedom.

I wondered if my relatives had joined the weekend exodus to West Berlin. Wolfgang was an electrician. He had done relatively well under the regime. He was even allowed to own his small business. He had something to lose. 'But never a member of the SED, let alone the Stasi!' my mother had pointed out. Repeatedly.

My father, a refugee from that part of German Silesia that was now Poland, would roll his eyes a fraction. 'Those East Germans always pretend they had nothing to do with the Nazis. They never had their moment of reckoning. I know they have had a miserable time but they have been granted an excursion from the past.'

My father was eleven at the end of the war. He was too young to be in the Hitler Youth. But he is proof that collective guilt can be very personal.

'Do you think that the two Germanies will ever be one?' I asked him in that November week.

'Doubt it. Very much doubt it,' he said. 'We have grown apart. We are different people. In any case, all they really want is the freedom to travel to Mallorca.'

My father was in West Berlin as a young reporter the day the Wall was built in 1961. He had been out drinking with a colleague and woke up hung-over on a park bench to find that he had broken his only pair of glasses. He found an optician's shop. It was jam-packed with people, all trying to buy binoculars. They needed them to see their relatives in the East, waving from windows, now stuck behind a wall. That was only twenty-eight years ago.

Once the East German border guards stood aside to let people walk or drive into what until that week had been a forbidden land, the flood became a stampede. 'Just for the weekend. Just to see what all the fuss is about.'

Trains in Lego colours were beached on the Ku'damm like abandoned toys. The queue outside the Aldi on Fasanenstrasse snaked round the block. East Berliners, wearing the kind of anoraks and stone-washed jeans that had stopped being fashionable in the West a decade before, emerged from sliding doors, grinning like winners at a gameshow, weighed down with shopping bags full of fresh fruit. Above all, fruit. Freedom meant fresh fruit.

The West German government had given every one of them 100 Deutschmarks on arrival. A welcoming present. 'Enough to buy a 1000 Kiwis,' one of them joked.

The queue outside the Dr. Mueller Sex Shop (the medical honorific provided a scientific alibi) on Kurfuerstenstrasse was even longer. They grinned here too. But it was a different kind of grin.

'Bananas and dildos, not to be confused. That's what they're after. That's what a free Europe is all about.'

The Grand Hotel Unter den Linden had only just opened. The authorities didn't even need to spell out that it was off-limits to anyone who wasn't a senior party member or sports celebrity. It was obvious.

The night the Wall was breached, *Sybille* magazine (East Germany's *Vogue*) was hosting a fashion show in the hotel's opulent atrium. Long-legged models swooped down to the broad, crescent-shaped staircase to polite applause and discreet nods from the audience of dignitaries. Crimean champagne was served in flat crystal coupes. There were mini blinis with real Russian caviar. The lobby belonged to another world. No one seemed bothered by the crowds of East Germans who were making their way to the Bernauer Strasse, crossing in the dense fog to see if the rumours were true. 'Instant exit visa. No waiting time. Just cross. The guards stand aside and watch. To the West. Incredible!'

No one in that lobby could know that they were witnessing the last edition of *Sybille* magazine. And with the last edition of everything else that had come to define their lives. All of it would be made to disappear: their party, their regime, their currency, their Stasi, their jobs, their status, their Crimean champagne, their fashion, their language and even their public memories.

East Germany was not to be mourned. It had been an ab-erration. An unpleasant phantom of a state. A year later, on the day of German unification, it would be declared extinct: a nation built on the victor's idea, and on a moment in history.

The moment had faded. The idea was dead. Trampled to

death by happy people bearing dildos and bananas. In the free Europe there was no room for an abhorrent abscess like East Germany.

I was halfway through writing my report when I heard the knock on the door. I made sure the dressing gown was properly belted and squinted into the spy hole. Through the distension of the tiny fish-eye lens I got a first warped glimpse of my alternative family history. My mother's cousin Wolfgang and his wife Christine and their two children. They were all wearing matching purple shell suits, like a family athletics team. I had never met them before. I knew so little about them. Now we were divided by a door. Did they know I was looking at them? I gave it another second and then opened the door to an awkward hello.

REFERENDUM

Lionel Shriver

LIONEL SHRIVER novels include *Sunday Times* bestseller *Big Brother*, the *New York Times* bestseller *The Post-Birthday World* and the Orange Prize-winning international bestseller *We Need to Talk About Kevin*. Her journalism has appeared in the *Guardian*, the *New York Times*, the *Wall Street Journal* and many other publications. She lives in London and Brooklyn.

Onlookers might have observed that everything worked out for the best, but one doesn't fall in love often in this life – not properly, anyway – and so far at twenty-nine Bitsy Littlewood could say with certainty that she'd taken the plunge only once. She met Simon Dunwell at a summer pub quiz at their local in Dulwich; starting out playing on the same team seemed symbolically propitious. He'd been impressed by her ability to rattle off what 'ERM' stood for and even to cite the year of Black Wednesday as 1992, despite her having been a toddler at the time. In retrospect, Simon had been *too* impressed, but that was the sort of perspective that one could only achieve with the benefit of romantic calamity.

In the context of the unironed, shirt-tail-out plaids and unintentionally distressed jeans of the competition, Simon was a snappy dresser. Suave, urbane, well travelled and multi-lingual, he intimidated her at first; he'd gone to Oxford, and his cultured parents were academics at Durham. He was one of those ahead-of-the-curve types who said 'woke' to mean 'right-on' before anyone knew what he was talking about, and who dropped the term like a hot brick once the trendy adjective began littering the text of balding, would-be-hip columnists in stodgy newspapers.

Admittedly, the dashing young man was domineering, although he was barely older than Bitsy, and had never stood on his own two feet as a wage-earning adult. But she'd still felt fragile at twenty-five, recently graduated and already carrying too much credit card debt. So she was grateful for his stabilising authority. He made her feel safe. His surety, his sense of mission, and his passionate engagement with grave international issues made her feel grander, more considerable and more caught up in the swing of things. If he was prone to think rather well of himself, that could only have meant that he had good reason. A tad shy and underconfident, Bitsy therefore received his attentions as a compliment. After all, the Littlewoods may have laid claim to a distinguished lineage, but the family had fallen on hard times since the war, and previously extensive holdings had shrunk to one farm. Conscious of these reduced circumstances and disinclined to boasting by nature, in this day and age Bitsy was hardly going to make a point of hailing from 'landed gentry'.

Bitsy was physically small, albeit nicely proportioned. Out of a combination of guardedness and pride, she'd always held herself a little apart from other people. To assertive men like Simon, that remoteness posed an irresistible challenge – to win her, to take her under wing, and thus to compromise the very autonomy that he found so attractive. She comported herself with a sensible bearing to which most suitors with an eye on the long-term would be drawn. Only an inborn practicality (why bother?) had prevented her from jettisoning her childhood's under-dignified diminutive of *Brittney* – especially since Simon sliced the nickname *Bitsy* to the bone. He meant it affectionately, but *Bit* seemed to threaten his girlfriend with such narrow existence that she was in danger of vanishing. Again, it was only clear in hindsight: there was a thin line between being enlarged by association and being swallowed up.

By the time the two began living together, Simon had enrolled in LSE, where he was earning an advanced degree in conflict studies (considering how matters panned out, perhaps a field in which he was less capable than he appeared at the time). No student was likely to pull his financial weight, especially with merely modest parental assistance and a stingy maintenance grant. So once Bitsy started full time at British Gas (a stretch for a conservation biology grad, but she fancied herself changing the system from within), she was proud to be the household's net contributor, which boosted her self-assurance and provided a pleasant sensation of magnanimity.

Simon was inevitably the more interested in politics. Likewise a Labour supporter, of course, Bitsy wasn't *un*interested in politics, but she was most engaged at the point where policy impacted regular life. So after (to her enormous relief) her best mate Gustav successfully used e-cigarettes to quit smoking, he complained about his pending inability to purchase 30-millilitre refills; only the puny 10-millilitre size would soon be for sale. EU regulations, he said. Bitsy commiserated: what good did that do? Tracking down cheap, offbeat lamps for the flat, she was dismayed to discover that the Oxfam in Streatham no long carried electrical goods; no one on staff had the newly elaborate qualifications required to replace a plug. EU regulations, they said. Or ordering more tooth-whitening gel, she was miffed when Amazon.co.uk no longer carried her regular brand – even if by then it was no longer a mystery why. Taken one by one, none of these inconveniences was especially grievous, but taken together (along with a great deal else), they betokened a gathering situation with which Bitsy was not altogether pleased.

But her boyfriend was the blue-sky type, who put great faith in institutions of noble purpose. While admiring Simon's high mindedness, she questioned lofty principles that didn't work in practice. This modest difference in sensibility fuelled many a convivial dinnertime conversation and powered them through to pudding. Indeed, when Bitsy accepted Simon's springtime proposal of marriage in the Prince Regent, he toasted wryly, 'To an ever closer union!' Back then, the crack was still funny. Because back then was still *before*.

It was glaringly obvious to them both – not to mention to the rest of the UK, and by the by to the whole world – that the Remain camp had the electoral upper hand. All right, strictly speaking, most polls were close. But the number of undecideds was massive: up to the wire, averaging about 15 per cent. Amid an innately cautious, small-C conservative polity, timid fence sitters were bound overwhelmingly to opt for the safer option – to choose, it was said, the devil they knew. 'Can you imagine,' Simon threw out rhetorically the night of 23 June 2017, 'not having made up your mind by the very day before, when the right answer is *that* obvious? A) Keep calm and carry on. B) Shoot self in head.'

So taking advantage of his decision to forego more than one referendum party – convocations that would merely mark the fact that nothing had changed were fated to feel anticlimactic – Simon got ready for bed on the early side. All that mattered was the point spread, he declared, and chances were high that a fair whack of these big-talking armchair reactionaries would also come to their senses at the last minute, sanity thereby prevailing at an even higher rate than the most optimistic polls had forecast. Wasn't that precisely what happened during the Scottish independence referendum two years earlier? A prudent preference for the status quo had proved just as surprisingly decisive. Voting having concluded only an hour before at 10 p.m., he could wait to hear either the cheerful or the *very* cheerful news in the morning.

'The sole merit of this ridiculous exercise,' he declared from the loo, worming his toothbrush with Colgate, 'is it's sure to fling the question into the long grass for generations. I bet there will never be another EU referendum in our lifetimes – or ever.' Once he'd brushed, Simon added, while poising a capful of mouthwash, 'Actually, the only ultimate *downside* to this farce? The Tories may finally stop ripping each other to shreds over Europe. That never-ending cat fight has been such a godsend.'

Bitsy was equally prepared to be bored by the result, but she was strangely wakeful (as opposed to *woke*) – both edgy and pensive. In the interest of domestic tranquillity, she'd been keeping her thoughts to herself. Oh, they'd obviously talked about it, even if Simon had done most of the talking. But she was uncomfortable with the implicit collusion of her quietude. Even now, she still hadn't decided whether to tell him. She didn't want to be laughed at, not by the man she was betrothed to wed. He might not cackle outright, but he would be head-pattingly patronising, and his best possible reaction would still be disagreeable: dismissing her with arch fondness as 'silly' or 'wacky' or a 'crackpot'. Yet they were contemplating a December wedding, and she was loath to sail into married life on the wings of a lie, even one of those sly, easy-to-get-away-with lies of simply keeping your gob shut.

Ruminating on the matter, she put her feet up in the sitting room, in front of *Sky News* with a bottle of bitter, and promised Simon to join him in bed once she got sleepy. But rather than start to nod off, once the first results came in from Newcastle – predicted to go for Remain, yes, but the vote was shockingly close, far more so than expected, at 49 versus 51 per cent – Bitsy returned her feet to the floor and craned forward on the sofa. When Sunderland followed quickly thereafter – forecast to go for Leave by about six points, but instead the spread in favour of going it alone was an astonishing *22 per cent* – she could barely tear herself from the screen to get another bottle of Black Sheep. Even the City's three-to-one Remain results couldn't dampen a rising effervescence, and as the early hours sifted on, to keep from waking Simon, she repeatedly stifled an urge to laugh. It turned out that she was living in a far more fascinating world than she'd hitherto imagined, in which anything could happen and sometimes did. By the time the light was greying out the sitting room windows, Bitsy was jumping up and down with a fist in her mouth and trying mightily not to shriek.

As Simon didn't have a class the next day until noon, Bitsy left for work before he got up. Not wanting to be a messenger he would wish to shoot, she left a neutral note whose meaning should only crystallise once he switched on his phone: 'Surprise, huh? B.' She ought to have been knackered, having stayed up all night – even when the final result was announced, she was too keyed up to even think about a couple of hours' kip – but instead she positively skipped through her day; it was like being on drugs. She was eerily immune to many a colleague's funereal gloom – leavened by unprofessional bursts of rage – as if she were wearing an emotional raincoat. The only downer loomed when she gathered her things to go home: if the unprintable not to mention uninterruptible lunchtime rant on her mobile was anything to go by, Simon was apt to be in a *somewhat different mood*.

Given the outcome, her small lie of omission had ballooned into a whopper, and Bitsy entered the flat with trepidation. *Get it over with ASAP*, she promised herself. Otherwise this low level nausea would accelerate, and she might actually be sick.

Simon was raging on his phone. Thank heavens he'd gone for a plan with unlimited minutes.

'This isn't going to happen,' he insisted. 'They're not going to get away with it. You don't allow a whole country to top itself . . . Let me count the ways! Parliament could intervene, or even the Lords – still packed with Blair's cronies. They're all pro-Europe. Or they'll hold another referendum, and if that doesn't work, another after that. Like the Lisbon Treaty. You just keep asking and asking the electorate, and they get tired. Eventually even cretins produce the right answer out of sheer exhaustion. Or most likely of all: we'll throw the animals a bone – like, some sorry-ass gesture of glorious patriotic independence. You know, like, *Look! Bully for you! You get to catch five more cod per year! Big ones, too!* And then we stay in the customs union, and the single market, and we quietly keep signing on to freedom of movement, and we're still in the EU for all practical purposes, but we *call it* something else, like 'semi-associate membership' or 'ancillary second-tier status once-removed' – some term all jumped up and arm's-length, the way you refer to cousins you're hardly related to. Meanwhile, business as usual. If I were Cameron, that's what I'd do – back in the days when there *was* a Cameron, like before this very fucking morning ... Yeah, I mean, really. What a coward. Can't stick around long enough to get soaked by the colossal wave of shite rolling towards Downing Street which that git *personally* set in motion. He broke the cardinal rule of politics, which isn't any different from the barrister's imperative in court: you *never* ask a question you don't know the answer to.' At last he glanced over at his girlfriend. 'Listen, this isn't helping. I'm giving myself a headache – a physical headache. And Bit just got home. I need to pretend to care.' He shot her a droll look, to bring her in on the joke.

But once he rang off, that was it for being amusing. 'You realise the pound has already tanked?' Simon charged. Bitsy took a step back. She hadn't even made her confession yet, and he was already acting as if the Leave vote were all her fault. 'If we took our life savings to France right now, we couldn't afford an order of *pommes frites.*'

'Ick anyway,' she said shakily. 'Chips with mayonnaise.'

Not even a half smile. 'The pound is just the beginning.'

'Good for exports,' Bitsy mumbled. For pity's sake, she felt like her mother: when in doubt, make tea.

'What exports? The biggest export on this rapidly sinking island is financial services. Which are now completely be-fucked. All those bankers in the City are packing for Frankfurt as we speak.'

'Seem like dodgy characters anyway,' she said, focusing fiercely on the kettle, lest the high-energy appliance 'overboil'. 'Good riddance.'

'That "dodgy" square mile ponies up *25 per cent* of the UK tax take.'

'Well, maybe pinching pennies will keep us from invading Iraq again.' Touché, but her tone was mousey.

Spurning her mother's universal palliative, Simon poured a pointedly sizable whisky – far too early in the evening and straight up, though he usually went for on the rocks. She wasn't convinced he wanted the drink. He wanted to *seem to need it*. She was picking up a lot of gesturing. His outrage was undercut by a crusading exhilaration.

'So what's with you, Bit?' Simon asked, making an ice-cube rattling motion that sloshed the neat whisky onto his hand. 'You don't you seem upset in the slightest.'

'You're upset enough for us both.' Shamefully, she was bottling it. 'I'm looking for the silver lining.'

'The lining, like everything else, is made of faecal matter! This country has just been hijacked by a rabble of racist, paranoid yokels with barely a secondary education. Overnight, they've turned Britain into an international pariah. Now the UK is officially one more bastion of pig-ignorant populism.'

She'd heard the term all day – long enough to take it apart. '*Populism* is just another name for *democracy* when you don't get your way.'

Simon shot her a sharp look of appraisal. She'd prepared

245

the *bon mot* on the tube. Though she was proud of it, the joust tipped her hand.

'You don't *seem* upset because you're *not* upset. I don't get it. I thought you were a serious person. This is the biggest, dumbest, worst thing to happen to our country in our lives, and you don't care.'

'I am serious, and I do care,' she said moderately, facing him with only Simon's ironic 'I-heart-Graphic-Clichés' mug to defend herself. 'But you're right: I'm not that upset.' She kept her tone offhand. 'I voted Leave.'

The prolonged beat of stupefied silence seemed awfully histrionic.

'You mean I am engaged to be married to a complete and utter plonker. A hopeless and irredeemable tosspot. A wally and a duffer and a bint.'

'Is that all?' she said sourly. 'You can do better than that. British synonyms for *idiot* are inexhaustible.'

'Little wonder. According to the referendum results, we have so many of them.'

'You're talking about me.'

'Yeah. Yeah, you bet. I'm talking about you.'

'I've been perfectly respectful of your position, so you might be a little more respectful of mine—'

'When you do something stupid, you're going to get called stupid. One of a host of reasons not to do stupid things. You and all your *stupid* little friends are going to have to own this, and you'll also have to own the whole cascade of catastrophes in the pipeline that you've brought down on *all* of our heads. From now to eternity your life is going to be one long I Told You So, and pretty soon all you self-destructive, inward, small-minded Little Englanders will be forced to wear a big scarlet *M* for Moron whenever you venture out in public – *if* you venture out in public, because you'll probably get lynched.'

'I looked it up this morning on Wikipedia: England is a thousand years old, and even the UK is three hundred—'

'Slow work day,' Simon said with a sneer.

'It was. Everyone was freaked out. But why? We've only been in the EU for forty of those years. So what makes being separate again so horrifying?'

'Because history doesn't run backwards.'

It seemed like just a thing to say, but she couldn't come up with a thing to say back; if she couldn't hold her own here, she'd get cornered into being pouty, obstinate, and girly. 'In any case,' she said with styled detachment, 'I told you a long time ago I had reservations.'

'*Reservations* are for a table for two at eight-thirty! This actually matters! Fuck your reservations!'

'I didn't take this vote casually, if that's what you mean.'

'Why didn't you come to me with your *reservations*? Christ, I thought you were just making conversation. Raising the odd point for the opposition, to keep our discussions from going flat.'

'Why didn't I come to you so that you could *tell* me how to vote? Simon Says? And then you could warn me that if I was *naughty* I'd brand myself as a "racist", like you said. Which is below the belt, and doesn't make any sense. The only immigrants up for grabs in the referendum yesterday were a bunch of other white people.'

'Standing on semantics.'

'We use words to mean something. That's why they're called *words* and not *sounds*.'

However briefly, Simon's eyes glinted with an appreciation for the fact that they might have the makings for a far fierier marriage than he'd imagined, but the light in his gaze no sooner appeared than it died. 'This has to do with your bumpkin Yorkshire family, doesn't it? They've tried to be polite and not pick fights when I've come with you to Beverley, but they're not good at hiding it: they're all Brexiteers. So it's the call of tribe. Daddy's voting Leave, so Bit falls into line. What a waste of adulthood. What a waste of *London*.'

He meant, of course, what a waste of Simon Dunwell.

'It's fucking hilarious, actually,' he added. 'Dairy farmers? Voting Leave? Without EU subsidies, your family's business would crater.'

'All that EU largesse is just giving us back our own money,' she said sullenly. 'Which I hardly need my parents to inform me.'

'Fair enough,' he said with exaggerated boredom. 'It's too late now, but for the record. Giving you the benefit of the doubt that this wasn't some thoughtless, knee-jerk, emotional self-indulgence – what was your *reasoning*?'

This was a total waste of time and doubtless just an exercise in self-humiliation, so she promised herself to keep it short, though she wasn't really a very concise person, and she probably wouldn't. 'At British Gas, every directive we have to comply with comes from the EU – never from our own government. And in the energy sector, there are scads of them. Like these smart meters, EU-mandated in every single home, but they're always breaking down, and often the readings are wrong – too high, naturally, especially if you use LEDs, which we've obviously been pushing like mad. We tell the customers the meters are "free", but that's a lie – the customers will pay for the whole rollout with higher energy bills. These gadgets don't actually achieve anything – they don't actually save energy – and after a few days the customers have figured out, right, the Dyson draws a lot of power, and ignore the readouts altogether. It's fake goodness, fake environmentalism—'

'Seriously,' he interrupted. 'Smart meters. You don't care for them, and that's why you've gone out of your way to destroy my professional future.'

'It's just – everywhere I go, whenever I run into some new rule, always about what you *can't* do or what you *can't* buy, it's always from the EU. It's like all these bureaucrats in Brussels do nothing but sit around all day thinking up new edicts in order to justify their bloated salaries.'

'Think you'd be in any more control of your destiny, and have any more influence on all those rules you resent, if you were governed solely from Westminster?' Simon countered incredulously. 'MPs are just as capable of justifying their existence by generating gratuitous regulations as the European Commission – better at it, in fact. Britain *invented* bureaucracy. I'm sick to death of hearing about the "democratic deficit" in Brussels. Democracy is a pantomime pretty much everywhere. At least benevolent dictators in Europe halfway know what they're doing, which is more than you can say for the spoilt Tory grandees knocking back cognac in the Commons bar who've never done a lick of real work in their lives.'

'I never knew you were such a cynic.'

'I never knew you were so unrealistic! You've always prided

yourself on being pragmatic. And if nothing else, picking apart EU legislation from the body of common law is going to take a small fortune, an army of civil servants, and about fifty years! It'll be like trying to separate your hairs from mine in the plughole.'

'Could you at least hear me out?' Bitsy said tremulously. 'To begin with, the EU was for the *mutual* benefit of its members. Now it's taken in all these poor, grubby countries in Eastern Europe—'

Simon snorted. 'And you don't think you're a bigot.'

'The point is, it's to *their* benefit to join, but not to ours. It's not a trading bloc any more, but a giant welfare programme. And the EU is too big, full stop. With all those unanimous votes, they can't make decisions. Look at the way they've dealt with the migration crisis – or failed to. What a Horlicks. Twenty-eight countries and they keep taking on more? And what's one of the next in the queue? *Albania*. Who does that help besides Albanians?'

'Jesus, are you collecting prejudices like stamps? What do you have against Albanians?'

'Nothing, but the original concept was to help the whole club, not to adopt dozens of charity cases. I'm sorry, because when it started out, with only those six member states, the European Union was a nice idea – but now it's unwieldy, and clumsy, and expensive, and bossy, and all about backhanders and jobs for the boys.'

'Any large organisation is going to be a little cumbersome and provide the odd sinecure,' Simon said wearily. 'That's no reason to slit your own throat.'

'And then there's freedom of movement,' she ploughed on.

'Which is brilliant in theory. But it only works with economies that are all, you know, sort of the same—'

Simon guffawed. '"Sort of the same"? That's the technical term?'

'I mean, a French engineer comes to build a bridge in London, and a British artist goes to paint in Paris. It doesn't work when the migration is all one way. Romanian wages are a quarter what they are in the UK. I'm surprised there's anyone left in Romania. We take all their young people and skilled workers and leave a bunch of old people and latchkey kids living on dribs wired back from abroad. While over here, we have no housing, the schools are bursting and none of the students speak English, and the NHS is collapsing . . .'

'My, my,' Simon said, clapping slowly with the wet sound of slapping dead fish. 'Someone's been talking loads to the mirror.'

'If I talk to the mirror, it's because my boyfriend isn't interested in what I think.'

'Economics has never been your strong suit, Bit. Those Romanians pick our strawberries and clean our hotel rooms. The tradesmen who do repairs to our flat are all from Poland or Bulgaria. You planning to take a plumbing course?'

'I don't want to live on a big blob of a continent lorded over by snoots nibbling on wild mushroom *vol au vents*. I want to live in a country.'

'Well, unless Westminster comes to its senses and shoves this whole debacle into reverse pronto, you'll get your wish. Your sentimental, irrational, short-sighted wish. You'll live in a *country* – which you can't leave, because you can't take a great job in Berlin any more because you can't get a work visa.

Your isolated, dumpy ex-empire will be a grotty shit hole with sky-high unemployment and rampant street crime, where your husband with a conflict studies degree can't find a job, either – since academic exchanges with the Continent and EU research grants will have all been cut off. Your kids won't get a decent education because the state can't afford to subsidise its universities, which used to be the *finest in the world*. Though at least I'll give you this much: foreign investors won't touch this place with a barge pole any more, so property prices will plummet, and at last we might be able to afford to buy a flat. There you are,' he signed off scornfully. 'Your *silver lining*.'

There are two kinds of bitterness: the kind that leaches away, and the kind that distils. Simon's was the kind that distilled – like a cup of black coffee left on a sill, until all that's left is acrid powder. Participation in the mass protest around Parliament Square the next day didn't get the acrimony out of his system, but worked him further into a lather. Some of his fellow Remainers claimed that London should secede.

Thereafter, he habitually exposed his girlfriend's Leave allegiance in public and held her backwards opinions up to ridicule. Among the younger set in London, Bitsy seldom stumbled across a fellow traveller, so she'd be left hanging her head on the margins as diners around a table took turns making snarky asides, taking cheap shots, or sometimes, with drink flowing, going all out with a red-faced harangue. In preference to the disembodied abstractions of newspapers and social media, they seemed to relish having captured in the flesh one of the throwbacks who had scuppered their career prospects and demoted them all to squalid little Britons instead of lofty, forward-looking, borderless Europeans. Whenever the company was a little older and thus less given to gory defenestration in restaurants, they regarded her as a rarefied zoo specimen, all but poking at her peculiar hide and touching her funny hair. Some seemed pleased with themselves for finally having 'met one', and they'd doubtless boast later about the extraordinary encounter with a mythological creature in chic London circles akin to the Loch Ness monster.

The couple's difference of opinion might have rounded into an affectionately needling running joke, which strengthened their relationship more than came between them. But their quarrel failed to gentle in this manner. Simon seemed determined to punish her, and to hold her accountable for anything unfortunate that happened, even turns of the wheel that had nothing to do with membership of the EU, and the burden was untenable. Not having been all that fiercely political for most of her life (even her environmental convictions were temperate), she would never quite puzzle it out; story-wise, it didn't make sense for her first true love to be sacrificed on the altar of a nationwide popular vote. But if his girlfriend had shown her true colours, Simon had also shown his, and in the end it was Bitsy who was obliged to call time.

Though she fancied the fairy-tale prospect of an amicable parting and would have liked to stay friends, Simon went out of his way to ensure such comity in future would be impossible. She'd never make it on her own, he railed. She was too dependent on him, and could never budget her finances or her time absent his more mature counsel. Remember all that credit card debt? Only Simon's discipline got it under control. Oh, and none of their mates would have anything to do with her without a witty, cosmopolitan partner to provide social clout, so she'd better get used to being alone. He portrayed her as flighty, weak and powerless. Though insulted, of course, Bitsy worried that there was truth to the depiction, and as the date neared by which she would shift to a meaner, more far-flung flat in the badlands of Croydon, she started having panic attacks. On more than one Gethsemane of an evening, she anguished over whether she might be making a terrible mistake. Perhaps she should beg his forgiveness for under-appreciating all that they had going for them as a team, renounce her ridiculous opinions, repent of her daft, childish impulse to flounce from his arms and implore him please, please to take her back.

Yet during the division their household, Simon betrayed a grasping side that made her wonder if all along he might have treasured her a tad too much for what couldn't even be called her generosity, when she'd never really been given any choice over picking up the financial slack. He insisted on keeping the white goods, which she had helped to buy. Meanwhile, in an effort to win over mutual friends to his side, he badmouthed her behind her back – playing up all the favours he'd done for her (what favours?) and casting her as an ingrate. Which raised the question of why, if she was roundly a disappointment, he was rancorous about having to let her go. Why wasn't he relieved instead? Maybe he thought it made him look bad, romantically, that some bumpkin from Yorkshire who worked for British Gas would willingly walk out on such a catch.

Because his parents had volunteered to co-sign, the lease was in Simon's name, so when their deposit was restored, it landed in his account. Though Bitsy had put up the whole two months' rent to secure the flat, he kept the entire packet – making some lame reference to its being part of their 'divorce settlement', when they'd never married after all. That put an end to her misgivings. Oh, she let him have the dosh (not that she was really given any choice on this dispensation, either). But on top of the contempt, the snide belittlement and the public disparagement – all the conniving, controlling and backstabbing – the bald avarice was the cherry on a pretty nasty sundae, and getting away from such a bully was worth the price.

WHAT THE WISE
MEN PROMISED

Jacob Rees-Mogg

JACOB REES-MOGG is the Conservative MP for the constituency of North East Somerset. Jacob sits on the Brexit Select Committee and the European Scrutiny Committee. After Eton, Jacob read History at Trinity College Oxford, before moving into finance. He now runs his own company, Somerset Capital Management, which specialises in investment management for pension funds and charitable organisations. Jacob's book on the Victorians will be published by WH Allen/Ebury (Random House) in May 2019.

*'What all the wise men promised has not happened, and what
all the damned fools said would happen has come to pass.'*
Lord Melbourne.

Leaving the European Union is a great liberation for the
United Kingdom, as worthy for celebration as victory
at Waterloo or the Glorious Revolution. It was a brave decision by an electorate that could not be cowed by prophecies
of doom by those who ought to have known better. It fits the
democratic spirit of the British and was a vote for freedom.

It was bold of the electorate to ignore the experts, for the
range of forces brought against the Leave campaign included
the President of the United States and a variety of international bodies, especially the IMF and the OECD. People do
not normally want to take an economic risk and although the
claims were spurious and have not transpired, even though
they were meant to happen immediately after the vote, they
were delivered by authoritative sources. Yet it chimed glori-
ously with Kipling's idea of the Saxon and the Norman:

'The Saxon is not like us Normans. His manners are not so
   polite.

But he never means anything serious till he talks about justice
    and right.
When he stands like an ox in the furrow – with his sullen set
    eyes on your own,
And grumbles, "This isn't fair dealing," my son, leave the
    Saxon alone.

It is not only a frame of mind that made the British suspicious
of the EU, it was also historic and constitutional differences. It
is not so much that as an island we have not been successfully
invaded, it is more that since the Civil War the land has not
been pillaged by ravaging bands of soldiers. On the Continent
the story is one of constant toing and froing, of armies leading to large scale displacement of people and a state that has
needed to be geared up to fight such battles. A more powerful
state with conscription and control on people's lives was necessary and became customary in these nations. The UK was
fortunate in that it did not see the need to maintain a large
army in peacetime and did not resort to conscription until the
middle of the First World War.

This ties in with constitutional differences which arguably
were in part created by the military needs. The first responsibility of the state is the security of its people, but if this can be
provided by limited powers then that is all that other powerful forces will allow to the rulers. Nobles do not want kings to
be too mighty unless their own land holdings depend upon it.
Thus England and later the UK has a constitution that grows
from the bottom up rather than from the top down. As Sir
John Fortescue, a Lord Chancellor to Henry VI, wrote the
King of England is the King under the Law while the King

of France is the Law. This has meant that the British government is controlled by ancient and unwritten conventions and has to govern by consent and always has done. Pitt the Elder could say in 1763 'the poorest man may, in his cottage, bid defiance to all the forces of the Crown. It may be frail; its roof may shake; the wind may blow through it; the storm may enter; the rain may enter; but the King of England cannot enter; all his forces dare not cross the threshold of the ruined tenement.' This is a model of liberty that the British held dear, but has never been the Continental way.

Common law reinforces the principle, a British person may do anything that is not specifically prohibited, there is no need to carry an identity card or to register an address with the authorities. Any restrictions that are placed are done so by consent via Parliament, which even before it was democratic represented interests and rejected excessive demands for power even from strong kings. It is worth remembering that the House of Lords neutered Henry VIII's Proclamations by the Crown Act 1539.

It is different from the civil code approach, which requires codified rights as powers reside with the state which may be delegated to individuals. The focus of the state above the individual is remarkably exemplified by the hereditary executioner in France, where one family held the post for six generations, from 1684–1847, cutting off the heads for the king and then of the king. The powerful state overrode outward forms of government. This type of state inevitably has a large number of regulations because they are needed to enable activity, whereas in the UK regulation stops things happening. The EU inevitably follows the Continental model as more of its members are civil law states.

Both systems can work, but imposing one on a nation used to the other is fraught with problems. In the top down states where rules govern everything, a system evolves of getting round them, such as the 'restaurant' in Rome I went to earlier in the year that was not licensed as such, so served its food with plastic knives and forks as this met the letter of the law. In a country where rules are made by consent there is a tendency to conform in an overbearing way, hence the metric martyrs. A system that is top down and heavily regulatory will only work in nations used to ignoring the state as otherwise it is too intrusive. In a consensual state used to following its own laws because the people have already bought into them this becomes unworkable, and this is why we found the EU impossible and slightly ridiculous.

Even the different voting systems in the UK and on the Continent change the relationship between the people and the rulers. Here the constituency system combined with first past the post creates a direct link and may lead to dramatic change. In proportional systems it is much harder to move away from the status quo, there is always some continuity in government regardless of what the voters have to say and those at the top of the list are secure in their positions. Grand coalitions are an anathema in the UK except in wartime but commonplace elsewhere, which is a great protector of the status quo.

Whether our system is better is a matter of opinion; I think it is, and it is why so many other of the world's most successful nations have adopted it. However, it is undeniably different, well rooted and supported by the British people. The institutions of the EU sought to overturn it and have failed.

THE WILL OF THE PEOPLE

Jonathan Lynn

JAMES GEORGE HACKER, Baron Hacker of Islington, KG, PC, Bsc (Lond.), Hon.DCL (Oxon.) was an academic political researcher, polytechnic lecturer and editor of a newspaper, *Reform*, before he entered Parliament. He continued his career in journalism while MP for Birmingham East.

For the first twenty years of his political career, Hacker was a member of the Opposition, and he served as Shadow Minister of Agriculture. Later he led the unsuccessful party leadership campaign of Martin Walker, who later went on to win the general election and thereby became prime minister. Hacker was nervous that he would be passed over for a cabinet post in revenge for running the campaign against the PM, but was appointed Minister for the Department of Administrative Affairs. At least one news commentator of the time speculated that the appointment was actually a poisoned chalice, as the DAA had a reputation as 'a political graveyard' that could end Hacker's career.

Hacker had to work with the ministry's Permanent Secretary, Sir Humphrey Appleby, the civil servant who controlled the DAA and tried to control the minister. Hacker received his third-class degree from the London School of Economics, and was frequently derided for this by the Oxford-educated Sir Humphrey. Hacker's Principal Private Secretary was Bernard Woolley, later Head of the Home Civil Service. Hacker and his wife, Annie, had one daughter, Lucy, by then a sociology student at the University of Sussex.

Hacker later gained an honorary doctorate from Baillie College, Oxford. He became Chairman of his party and subsequently 'emerged' as Prime Minister in an internecine leadership struggle master-minded by Sir Humphrey. After Hacker eventually left Number Ten he was elevated to the House of Lords, and his last job was Master of Hacker College, Oxford, a new college named after him.

JONATHAN LYNN wrote the bestselling books *The Complete Yes Minister* and *The Complete Yes, Prime Minister*, based on the multi-award-winning BBC series, created and co-written with Antony Jay. The books sold more than a million copies in hardback, were translated into numerous languages and are still in print nearly thirty years later. Other books: his new novel *Samaritans*, the novel *Mayday* (to be republished in December) and *Comedy Rules*.

His eleven films as writer and/or director include *Clue*, *Nuns on the Run*, *My Cousin Vinny*, *The Distinguished Gentleman*, *The Whole Nine Yards*, and he has written and directed two successful plays seen in London. Awards: BAFTA Writers Award, Writers Guild (twice), Broadcasting Press Guild (twice), NAACP Image Award, Environmental Media Award, Ace Award (Best Comedy Series, US cable) and a Special Award from the Campaign For Freedom of Information.

Reflections upon leaving Europe, dictated by the Lord Hacker of Turnham Green, shortly before his demise.

[A note from the editor: This recently discovered entry in the diaries of the legendary former Prime Minister, the Right Hon. Jim Hacker MP, was transcribed from recordings he made on his iPhone shortly after he was ensconced as the first Master of Hacker College, the academic institution named after him at Oxford. We publish it after careful consideration, concerned that revealing his confused mental state may not be the best thing for his reputation, casting doubt as it does on his capacities as one of the Great and the Good at this late stage in his life. While it is true that he had always shown signs of delusional thinking and slight cognitive impairment, these had been construed as essential for a successful career in politics. So although such a fragment would usually be excised from the traditional political memoir, we feel, on balance, an obligation to reveal, in full, the words that shed light on the sad conclusion to a remarkable career.]

This Brexit thing really is an awful headache. Before the referendum I was in favour of Remain . . . at least, I think I was. Now I'm in favour of Brexit . . . well, I think I am.

But I'm a bit reluctant. I love Europe. I love Paris in the springtime. Wonderful, wonderful Copenhagen. Brussels . . . sprouts. Roman blinds, Spanish Steps, Romanian Rhapsody,

Czech-mate, French kisses ... What a romantic continent! How can we desert them in their hour of need?

Or is this *our* hour of need? Hard to tell.

I always believed wholeheartedly in the European Common Market as a way to end all those devastating Continental wars, by creating an overriding economic interest in each other's survival. Much better than an overriding interest in each other's destruction. But everything in moderation: some said turning that market into a vast federal state with about thirty-five official languages was a bridge too far.

We renounced so much: we gave up our yards for metres, our pints for litres. Pints! That was our heritage, really. We lost the sixpence and the shilling. I weep for the ha'penny and the thrupenny bit, the florin, the half-crown. Gone the way of all flesh. [*Sounds of weeping on the tape – Ed.*] And what the hell is 10 degrees Celsius? I heard it on the wireless this morning and had to look it up! It's 50 degrees Fahrenheit – a nice English summer's day. Or used to be, in the old days.

We made all these sacrifices for international goodwill, but, finally, we do need to gain control of our border and our own currency. [*The UK already had both, of course, before Brexit. Hacker seems to have forgotten this – Ed.*]

I think the problem is the whole hard Brexit versus soft Brexit thing. It's like a boiled egg. While they're discussing whether it would be better hard or soft, it's gone rotten. Something is rotten in the state of Brexit. But *what* is rotten: Brexit or Europe? That is the question.

We don't really know what the Europeans are thinking, because we have to rely on the civil service for translations. I'm sure the PM doesn't know much German or French beyond *Sprechen sie Englisch?* and *Zum flughafen, bitte* or *Gott in Himmel!* ['*Do you speak English?*' And '*To the airport, please*'. '*Gott in Himmel*' *needs no translation, we believe – Ed.*]. As for her French, I think *Je ne parle pas Français* or *Taisez-vous!* ['*Shut up!*' – *Ed.*] covers it. She has a degree in geography, but so what? Geography is easy, because it never changes. Unless there's a war. Then the winners change the borders, which leads to the next war.

Economics, which I studied, is quite different. The questions keep changing. And if the questions don't change, the answers do. That's why no one ever has any idea what to do in an economic crisis. It's always new.

Everyone says we can't turn back. Can't we? I decided to consult Humphrey, my old adversary and companion-in-arms – to tell you the truth, I was never quite sure which – because he *does* know his constitutional law. Or did before his move to St Dymphna's Home for the Elderly Deranged. And even now, he can't possibly be more deranged than the current cabinet or shadow cabinet.

'Humphrey,' I began, because that's his name, and I thought I'd better remind him, in case he'd forgotten, 'everyone says that we must Brexit because it's the will of the people. The people have spoken.'

Humphrey said, 'They have indeed, Prime Minister. But I don't see why they can't speak again. After all, it might perhaps be somewhat preferable if the populace were to expatiate only if and when they exhibited, and were able to articulate, sufficient proficiency, capability and verbal dexterity to handle the inscrutability of this diplomatic perplexity.'

'Come again?' I said.

'It would be better,' he said, 'if the people knew what they were talking about before they spoke.'

'Is there any argument against that?'

'Well . . . yes and no. It could be argued that knowing what one was talking about could create a dangerous precedent. On the other hand, politicians have always spoken from a position of nearly total ignorance, so perhaps it is appropriate for the people to emulate their leaders.'

'Whether or not they knew what they were talking about,' I said, 'the will of the people was expressed in that vote. That can't be changed.'

'Why not?' asked Humphrey. 'The will of the people is expressed every five years or so in a general election. If the people weren't allowed to change their minds there would never need to be any more elections.' He paused. 'Which might not be such a bad thing, by the way.'

I began to think that it's not such a bad thing he's in a home.

'Let's face it,' he went on, 'very few of the people had any grasp of what they actually voted for.'

'Nothing new there,' I said.

'The Leave campaign said the referendum was just advisory. They said it wouldn't be binding. But that was when they thought they'd lose. When they won, it became binding after all!'

'Yes,' I agreed. 'You must admit, they handled that rather well.'

'Prime Minister, you telephoned me for my opinion on constitutional law, not unscrupulous politicians. Let me explain the novel situation in which we find ourselves.' [*Describing the situation as novel was an indication of Sir Humphrey's profound disapproval of the way the referendum had been handled – Ed.*]

'Go ahead,' I said.

'We used to have a parliamentary democracy,' Humphrey said. 'We never used to ask ordinary people what they thought about constitutional issues. That's not the British tradition. It was none of their business. No, once a government was in power, they said "We have a mandate," and went and changed the constitution if they felt like it. Like that little man Blair did with the Lords reform and devolution. They argue that when we leave Europe we'll regain our sovereignty. Then they say that our sovereignty depends on a sovereign parliament. And *then* they say "The sovereign parliament can't vote to Remain, because it would be obstructing the will of the people." Doublethink!'

'So what do you suggest?' I asked.

'The government has not taken on board the complexity of unwinding forty years of regulatory activity. Extricating ourselves from the European Union is a Herculean and Brobdingnagian task – indeed one might almost say Cyclopean. Though the political leaders of this sceptre'd isle may be expert in matters of intrigue, chicanery, subterfuge and distortion, all undeniably useful attributes in a negotiation of considerable complexity, it is demonstrably and unarguably true that to face simple reality is beyond the capacity of the delusional political principals to whom the people entrusted the management of this situation, who may have proven skills in duplicity and concealment but not, unfortunately, in the essential comprehension, confirmation, validation and notification to the British public of much disagreeable and indeed unacceptable information.'

'What?' I said.

'What do you mean, "what?"' he asked.

'I mean what? Put it in plain English.'

'I don't see how it can be any plainer,' he said. 'But, grossly simplified: Get rid of the politicians. Throw the bums out. Is that plain enough?'

'Which politicians?' I asked.

'All of them! Squalid vote-grubbers who'll do anything for short-term electoral advantage or for the sake of party unity – as if anything could matter less. Get thee gone, the lot of you!'

'Don't be ridiculous,' I said. 'Who would run the country?'

'It may seem like a revolutionary thought, but how about people who are *qualified*. People who are *sound*?'

'You mean, *you*.'

'Yes. Or someone like me.'

'That *would* be a precedent,' I said. It's a good thing he's in a home. I hope he's in a locked ward. I rang off without another word.

I considered my position. After I retired from Number 10 [*Was pushed out ignominiously – Ed.*] and I graciously accepted a peerage, I chose to sit on the cross benches in the Lords. And when it comes to Brexit, some of us *are* pretty cross. But I still have a vote, and it is clear to me that we should stay in Europe. So I'll be voting for Brexit, like everyone else. I can't be seen to be against the will of the people. As one of their leaders, I must follow them.

So it's goodbye to all that. The lights are going out all over Europe. Or, maybe, all over Britain.

Not sure.

OI, FARAGE! LITTLE BRITAIN: HOW VERY DARE YOU?

Robert Crampton

ROBERT CRAMPTON, fifty-three, is a journalist who has been writing for *The Times* for twenty-six years. Interviewer, feature writer, editorialist and reporter, he is perhaps best known for 'Beta Male', his long-running column in the *Saturday Magazine*, a collection of which offerings was recently published in book form. As Robert's contribution to this volume strives to make clear, despite proudly possessing many of the attributes of what some might erroneously consider to be the archetypal characteristics of a classic Little Englander, he is nonetheless defiantly on the side of his beloved country remaining part of the European Union.

I voted Remain. So did my wife and my son. My daughter would have too, but she was only seventeen at the time. The morning after, she was in tears. 'They've fucked up my future,' she sobbed, 'and they'll all be fucking dead in ten years anyway.' I wouldn't normally allow Rachel to make so free with expletives, but on this occasion I cut her some slack. Not least because her outburst was, in my view, a pretty decent summary of the referendum result. Plus, I felt sorry for the girl.

Later that same day, I saw my friend and neighbour Sapan, whom despite being born and raised in Ealing I guess would be categorised as Anglo-Indian. 'So,' Sapan said, partly ironically but partly not, 'you don't really want us here after all, do you?' I've rarely felt so ashamed.

The odd epoch-defining exception apart, I am no sort of a liberal, in my parenting approach or otherwise. I'm pretty trad in many respects. I may live in what critics are pleased to call the metropolitan media bubble, but it's supposed mores do not define me. It's not where I'm from, nor is it somewhere I feel particularly comfortable. Sure, most of my colleagues, friends and relatives voted to stay in the EU – a significant minority, however, did not. While I live in Hackney, east London (78.5

per cent Remain), my formative years were spent in Hull, East Yorkshire (67 per cent Leave). Much of my family is spread around the planet, much of it is concentrated in the same spot I grew up in.

In recent months, reading about Jean-Claude Juncker and this new chap, what's his name, Michel Barnier, dissing our people, my instinct is to tell these guys to fuck the fuck off. Not very grown up, I know. And yet, channelling my inner Richard Littlejohn, it's the way I feel. As regards the emotions going on – and the vote on 23 June 2016 was nothing if not emotional, it was in fact a gigantic nationwide emotional spasm – I get it. When I read stories in the *Daily Mail* about how barmy Brussels bureaucrats are conspiring to straighten our sausages (oo-er missus!) my visceral reaction is to line up loyally behind bendy British bangers.

Which is to say, for what's it's worth, while acknowledging the brutal binary division that sundered my country last summer, I wholly reject that division. As I hope many of us would. I think Brexit will be a disaster, but I don't despise the people who made it happen. I'm connected to Middle England, provincial Britain, the so-called silent majority, call it what you will. I share many concerns regarding pompous politicians from the Low Countries. Or (even worse) France.

What's more, I think Samuel Johnson was wrong about patriotism being the last refuge of a scoundrel. I don't disagree with Cecil Rhodes oft-derided dictum that to be born English is 'to have drawn first prize in the lottery of life'. I'm not so sure about 'my country, right or wrong' or E.M. Forster preferring to betray his country as opposed to his friend – obviously they're both a little more nuanced and dependent on context – but you get the general idea. I'm reasonably well travelled, but I've never been anywhere else I'd rather live than right here.

Although I have to say Tuscany, the Dordogne, the New England states of the US and much of Scandinavia all have their merits. Antigua is pretty lovely as well.

All that said, when Nigel Farage claimed the Leave vote as a victory for 'ordinary decent people', with the clear implication that those of us who'd voted to Remain were peculiar indecent people, in some way weird, in some way denatured, in some way deracinated, in some way unpatriotic, it made my stomach churn. I find that statement very hard to forgive. Not least because it demonstrated a singularly unBritish intolerance for the opposing view.

I say that as someone who, impeccably conciliatory Englishman as I am, much as I might disagree with his views, has a certain affection for Farage. Hell, I like a pint and a fag myself. And besides, the guy's a laugh, right? Like him or loathe him, you can't deny he's authentic. There are plenty of Brits like Nige. They're not entirely my cup of tea, but hey, it's a big tent, a mongrel nation, all sorts are welcome. As a bona fide patriot, I wouldn't wish to exclude Nigel Farage any more than I would an asylum seeker fresh into Heathrow from Kurdistan.

How dare he say that? How dare he? I don't want to labour the point. But just for the record, having researched that record, my family – on both sides, going back as far as I can trace it – have been here on this island for a long, long time. Rather longer – and I resent getting in such a nativist competition, but it feels necessary – than have the families of many of the most prominent Leave advocates. Several centuries, as far as I can tell. Living, dying, farming, labouring, fighting, mining, preaching, teaching, writing. Cramptons served at Trafalgar and Waterloo. My granddad was at Gallipoli. My great uncle won the Croix de guerre in France in 1917.

Big deal. So what. Lots of other people's forebears did the same thing. I shouldn't have to establish my credentials like this, but the way last summer's campaign panned out, and given Farage's subsequent comment, I don't have any choice. It was a shockingly divisive process, made infinitely worse by the victor's decision to question the legitimacy and identity of those of us who lost.

That vote was quite the silliest, stupidest act of national self-mutilation I've observed in my lifetime. I hope it doesn't cost us too dear, I hope we'll be able to mitigate the worst effects, culturally and economically. I'm hopeful it'll all be all right in the end – I doubt there'll always be a Britain, but I'm confident there'll always be an England. And people like me will be a part of it. We ain't going anywhere.

DISCOVERING EUROPE

Yasmin Alibhai-Brown

YASMIN ALIBHAI-BROWN was exiled from her birthplace, Uganda, in 1972. She is a journalist, author and academic. She has written for the *Guardian*, *Observer*, *Sunday Times*, *Mail on Sunday*, *Daily Mail*, *New York Times*, *Time Magazine* and was a weekly columnist for the *Independent* for eighteen years. She is now a columnist for the *i* newspaper, *International Business Times* and the *New European*. She has won several awards including the Orwell prize for political writing and National Press Awards columnist of the year prize. Her last book, *Exotic England*, explored England's love of the east. She is a part time professor at Middlesex University. And a great cook.

This is a tale of transformation, from inherited historical prejudices to new awakenings, from distrust to ardour, from a wince to a kiss. None of it was planned. I was unaware of the shifts myself until the EU referendum, when my country, Britain, ruptured, erupted like a volcano that had long been inactive and safe. The English Channel became wider, wider until it was an uncrossable, salty ocean, separating us from them. And I finally came to understand how much EU nations, colours, languages, cultures, diversities and histories, meant to me. Goodbye Europe. My love for you flared up at an impossible time. I will never get over you.

I was born in lush Uganda, a British protectorate between 1894 and 1962. At school we were inculcated with aggrandising, nationalistic narratives, which, looking back, seem preposterous.

Shakespeare swept his audiences off to Venice and Rome, Egypt and magic (un-English) kingdoms; Byron found peace and renewal in Sintra and various European centres of artistic splendour, Charlotte Brontë (as well as Emily) taught English in Belgium and learned French; that quintessentially English painter, J.M.W. Turner was moved by the landscapes of Switzerland and Italy. Everyone who was anyone went on the

Grand Tour. Yet we, impressionable, colonial saplings were taught Brits were greater than other Europeans. That Spaniards were iniquitous, Italians were unruly and fascistic, the Dutch were bigoted and Portuguese pathetic. That Germans were the foulest of all, irredeemably evil and militaristic.

We memorised John of Gaunt's 'This sceptre'd isle' speech from *Richard II*. I won a tin of Walker's Nonsuch Toffees for reciting Tennyson's 'Britons, Guard Your Own' during assembly.

'Vive l'Empereur' may follow by and bye;
'God save the Queen' is here a truer cry.
God save the Nation,
The toleration,
And the free speech that makes a Briton known.
Britons, guard your own.
Rome's dearest daughter now is captive France,
The Jesuit laughs, and reckoning on his chance,
Would, unrelenting,
Kill all dissenting,
Till we were left to fight for truth alone.
Britons, guard your own.

The colonial system, like apartheid, was based on a racial hierarchy: whites were at the top, Asians were below them and Africans at the very bottom. And yet, we, the children of the subjugated, cheered the triumphs of our masters. It was a quite a miseducation.

In 1962 British rule ended. After my A levels, I went to Makerere, a globally rated university. This was the heady post-colonial era, when intellectuals and activists defied Western hegemonies and went through a process of deconditioning. Négritude, the French-African anti-colonial literary movement, influenced us as did writers such as James Baldwin, Wole Soyinka and Mulk Raj Anand. Inexplicably, while the head was liberating itself, the foolish heart still remained faithful to the old masters. My father, Kassam, an Anglophile who dressed like Graham Greene, said 'the good days' were gone. The future was bleak.

In 1972 Asians were thrown out of Uganda by Idi Amin. The UK had just joined the EC (European Community), a sign of old enmities being laid to rest. I got into Oxford! The joy and optimism didn't last long. The ethos was cloying and smug. I lost my fighting spirit. A centrifugal force sucked me into Little England. I wore Laura Ashley dresses, made scones and listened to Steeleye Span. By 1978 I felt fully assimilated.

Europe felt foreign and alienating. I went across on trips but didn't warm to the French, thought Spaniards were capricious, Greeks surly, Swiss stiff and cold, Portuguese feudal and regressive. Those old British school teachers had done a fine job. They had made me into a keen xenophobe.

After Oxford I taught refugees and migrants from South America, Iran and the Lebanon for a few years. Then, in 1978, I got a job teaching English as a foreign language at a posh school in Holland Park, London. Some of the students lodged in my flat. Among the many who passed through were Swiss bankers, Italian designers, Swedish journalists and Japanese businessmen. We got close. Marcello invited me to Venice, Sven to Stockholm, Maria to Barcelona. Leonello from Genoa was sweetly romantic; Birgit, a Swiss lesbian, flirted outrageously;

a Greek couple, Olivia and Dmitri, became dear friends. Intimacy pushed out preconceptions about most Europeans but not the French and Germans. In rural France, I had experienced burning racial hostility. They seemed to despise Arabs and other dark-skinned people. With Germans the problem was me, not them. They were installed in my head as real baddies. I didn't go to Germany, didn't have German student lodgers. Shameful and unforgivable.

I became a journalist, travelled across Europe. In 1993 I was invited to speak at the University of Freiburg on race relations in the UK. My baby daughter was still breastfeeding. It was my first trip to Germany. A kindly old couple looked after her, gave her a beautiful old doll and a music box. At the Christmas market, strangers bought her a dinky hat, asked to hold her, my black-eyed, brown girl. Germans I met did not shirk from examining their demonic past and were passionate anti-racists. In 1994 I went to Berlin, where they were managing both reunification and a rise in migration. Neo-Nazis, nervous monoculturalists and the jobless were restive but the leaders kept their heads. I came away thinking post-war Germany was one of the most civilised and humane of nations.

This Little Englander became an instinctive internationalist. I felt I truly belonged in London, the cosmopolitan metropolis, world emporium. Remember how we felt during the 2012 Olympics? Where did all that go?

Britain has entered a period of savage intolerance and isolationism. European citizens, the dispossessed, Commonwealth immigrants, lefties, internationalists, social democrats and liberals are seen as 'enemies of the people'. A woman spat at me on the bus in November 2016. Told me to 'fuck out' of her country. I would if I could. Maybe go live in Berlin. Or Barcelona. Can't do that. So I must grow old in these shrunken isles. I lost one homeland and am lost in the one I found.

LOVE LETTER TO LANGUEDOC

Kate Mosse

KATE MOSSE is an internationally bestselling novelist, essayist & playwright, the author of six plays, three works of non-fiction and eight novels, including the multimillion selling *Labyrinth* and the Gothic thriller, *The Taxidermist's Daughter*. Co-Founder of the Women's Prize for Fiction, and host of the pre/post interviews with directors, actors and writers at Chichester Festival Theatre, Mosse is also Deputy Chair of the National Theatre. *The Burning Chambers* – the first novel in a new major historical series set in Carcassonne, Toulouse, Paris Amsterdam & South Africa and spanning three hundred years (from 1562–1862) will be published in May 2018. She divides her time between West Sussex and Languedoc, southwest France.

Returning to Languedoc after some time in self-imposed exile, I found myself making the same journey either side of the Brexit referendum. Reflecting on those two trips a year apart, much has changed. My new novel – the first in *The Burning Chambers* series – is done and dusted, and the sheer folly of Brexit – an act of unparalleled national self-harm, brought about by arrogance, incompetence, dishonesty – has, in the space of fourteen months, unleashed an alarming level of xenophobia and ugliness.

Leaving aside the financial consequences (severe), the optimism (suffocated), the opportunities (reduced), the offence to common sense (obvious), what does Brexit mean for any of us who live a half-and-half existence? Who feel connected with a country other than our own – as visitors, as writers, as parents, as daughters-in-law, as travellers?

2016: Friday 10 June

There is a joy in arriving slowly, with the pace of the sun, feeling the air on your face. An immersion, a remembering of all the things that speak of place: texture of the light, distinctive smells, the scuff of the pavement beneath one's feet.

Over the nearly thirty years I've been travelling from Toulouse to Carcassonne, my journey has become less rushed. I take the *navette* from the airport, Blagnanc – where, more than 300 years ago, the Huguenot armies mustered before the massacre of Toulouse – to the railway station. Having been a carer for the past five years, I have not done this journey for a while. What's different? At Matabiau, a cluster of police with machine guns at the door. Calm, laughing with students, all rather sleek and glamorous, ponytails and tangs – straight out of Hollywood Central Casting.

Rather than the train, for this first writing trip I take the autocar. Two-and-a-quarter hours, 16 euros for a *billet simple*. My notebook and rucksack, a bottle of water and a *sandwich mixte* (with the ham discarded) and I feel like a traveller. Unburdened. Free, with all the time in the world.

And, what? Thinking to jolt my creative brain into action by immersing myself in the Midi. I'm writing about the sixteenth-century Wars of Religion, the sequence of eight wars – punctuated by periods of armed and uneasy peace – that brought France to her knees. I wonder if my protagonist, Minou, will make this journey when the novel starts in 1562, but I don't know. What I do know is that on this long and jolting journey I will map the land between the two cities and see if it starts to sing. I feel excited, though peaceful. I open my notebook, write in capital letters: HERE!

I board the autobus at 12 noon. There are only a few of us, but minutes before it is due to leave at 12.15, there's a rush. French, Arabic, English, the smart, the down on their luck, students and backpackers. The seats fill. The smell of sweat and travel, fizzy drinks.

My notebook is on my lap, the letters jolted by the motion of the bus. The throbbing of the engine, then a slow pulling away and we're following the Canal du Midi. I think of Larkin's *The Whitsun Weddings*, which fits so perfectly the polite, slightly awkward atmosphere of strangers linked by nothing but the experience of sharing a particular journey, on this particular day.

Montraudan is first, a shabby, down-on-its-uppers suburb with a traveller site. Old-fashioned white caravans, then wooden shacks with corrugated iron roofs. A French shanty town, but in the Toulouse suburbs. A street called Rue Lecrivain; I wonder if it means 'the writer', or is simply someone's surname.

Later, I learn that this is sold as one of the key aerospace suburbs – they cite all the great aviators, including Saint-Exupéry – so, odd connection. It doesn't look of the next century; sadly, now – with Calais, Lesbos, Jordan, it looks of this. At Lalande, two young backpackers get on in the middle of an industrial park. I wonder where they've come from to be boarding here. Are they coming or going?

Labège-Innople, a high tech city, is next, then suddenly we are out into the light green of spring – May trees, oak, silver birch, dark firs.

We pass travellers setting up a funfair, rides in huge metal sections ready to be bolted together. Escalquens, a very local name, though the slope to the left of the road looks like a Sussex hillside.

We stop at La Cousquille and there are pink and white blossoms, a long straight drive and an incongruous Loire chateau *domaine*. I'd like to find out who built it, and when, but I know I'll forget.

The fields are bright, the colours primary. Blocks of blue, green, yellow, like a child's painting. Then, Villefrance-de-Lauragais. Familiar from writing *Labyrinth* a decade ago, but I can't remember why. Too many other facts, stories, imagined characters, have got in the way.

The road runs to the east of the motorway. Several passengers get off at the SNCF station at Baziège. A sweet red-brick building and a pretty town with a *cloche mur*. On a different day, I might get off and explore, but it's enough to look from the windows.

At Villenouvelle, the houses to either side of us have twin sets of stone steps leading up to high front doors. I sketch a picture. And, still, everywhere yellow and green. Chickens in a garden and suddenly – miraculously – a glimpse of the Pyrenees between the buildings. Snow on the highest peaks? Still? Cragged rock set clear in a blue sky.

I don't write HOME! Though, reading these notes later, I wonder why not. That first glimpse is always so utterly the beginning of stories. I see signs to Avignonet and I remember the murder of two Inquisitors during the Cathar Crusades in 1242, and the legend of their skulls being used as drinking vessels. The point of the story was that what appeared to be a victory for the defenders of the Midi was in fact a catalyst for the final, violent engagement. The siege of Montségur from 1243–44, and the end of the independence of the Midi.

I wonder if any of these places will feature in my new series of novels. An odd obelisk set on a hill, which I will investigate. This is the true nitty-gritty of writing. Once the library research is done, the book research done, it's the picking up of the threads of story within the landscape. Time, place, fact are kissing cousins to plot and character.

Two birds of prey circle. Buzzards, hawks? Otherwise, the fields are deserted. Nobody working in the fields, no animals on the roads, just an occasional car.

Blue shutters. Elsewhere, it is the launch of Euro 2016 and France is the host country.

What a stupid day to travel. What a glorious day to travel.

2017: Friday 30 June

Days pass, the Referendum. Months pass, a year. The truth of Brexit – or at least the muddle of it – becomes clearer and clearer. The scientific research jeopardised, the farmers' subsidies squandered, the international students and nurses deterred, the artists not invited, the security data not to be shared, the 'divorce' bill gigantic, the lies. Most of all, the lies.

On the autobus again, with water and the same sandwich, and what's changed? The same journey, but a different landscape? Is it? I feel different, but does the Brexit vote influence how I write or feel or engage, beyond border controls and customs and a sense of embarrassment? Inconvenience is not suffering. And in Languedoc, an area of France where so often they have stood firm and alone against their government's edicts, there is the sense that 'the politicians are at it again'. The reality, of course, is that although the UK feels itself to be at the heart of things, everywhere else in Europe we are on the outskirts.

The coach rattles and belches through the outskirts of Castelnaudary, then on across the border of Haute-Garonne into Aude. This is a soft border. In Pexiora, a long vapour trail high in the sky that fizzles out. Again, the Pyrenees. Astonishing, clear, contoured.

Into Bram, where, in 1210, the Crusaders blinded all the men, leaving only one to lead them from the walled town, as a lesson to others who might resist. Are we Englishers now, in 2017, to resist? The station is disappointingly drab, ordinary, a dead end street. No one leaves. No one joins. The coach stops, turns, waits and moves away.

The novel is finished, just needs the finishing touches. The polishing and the knocking off the sharp edges. I look at my watch; it won't be much longer before we are in Carcassonne. Jumbling through the *banlieues* towards the Bastide. Across Boulevard Barbès, past the Bastion du Calvaire, heading to the terminus at the top of the town.

We swoop and turn into the loading sheds of the SNCF in Carcassonne. I think of the next book in *The Burning Chambers*. How, at the tail end of the sixteenth century, the Cité and the Bastide declared for different sides in the Religious Wars: the medieval citadel staunchly Catholic, and the modern town, of commerce and business, giving their allegiance to the Huguenots. Is that where we are now? Them on one side, us on another?

No words are spoken as we disembark, each of us released to our own lives. Bright sunshine, fierce wind, boats on the Canal du Midi. The Hotel Terminus looks the same.

Later, when I ask what friends in Carcassonne think about Brexit, they simply shrug. As if to say they are not surprised. There are more soldiers on the street – after the horrors of Bataclan and Nice – but they are no less glamorous. The Place

Carnot feels the same. The bells ring for Mass, as they always did. The accordion player squeezes out his same old tunes.

This then, I suppose, is it. That governments often do the wrong thing for their citizens. They confuse self-interest with what is best for the country they claim to serve. At the same time, walking through the new town towards the Pont Vieux, the echoes of the stories as yet unheard, unwritten, are not changed by London or Brussels. I feel the atmosphere of autumn, the end of something. But no one else cares.

Perhaps this is the saddest feeling of all. That life here will go on perfectly well without us.

ANCHORS AND FIGUREHEADS

Marie Le Conte

MARIE LE CONTE is a French-Moroccan writer living in London. She grew up in Nantes and moved to the UK aged seventeen to study journalism then never left. Since then, she has worked for a range of publications including the *Evening Standard* and *BuzzFeed*, and her writing mostly focuses on politics and current affairs.

I never thought I'd complain about being pushed too far into the spotlight. I enjoy attention, as I suppose most do, and if a certain event means that my opinions become more popular than they should be, I will cherish the moment and enjoy it while it lasts.

I will enjoy it even more if it comes after some months during which my point of view was neither needed nor wanted, and I was left to watch the country I call home tear itself apart without asking for my permission.

I moved to London in 2009 as a voracious teenager, and saw England not as a real country but as a slightly irascible playground I'd got to know through the books and songs and movies I'd grown obsessed with in France.

Over the following six years I rarely stopped to think about my feelings towards the United Kingdom and what I wanted my position to be. I had, after all, moved by packing up a suitcase and buying a one-way Eurostar ticket, and hadn't been burdened by much bureaucracy along the way.

This, of course, changed when David Cameron announced that he would be calling a referendum on the UK's membership of the European Union, and by January 2016 there was little else to talk about.

Watching someone go through an identity crisis is a bit like yawning – it'll inspire you to do the same, whether you want it or not. And so, as the UK struggled to find its place in the world and decide what kind of country it wanted to be, I was forced to retreat and think about my own predicament.

These two processes happened alongside each other, but rarely crossed – I, and others like me, were very much made to feel like our opinions did not matter or, worse, could swing good honest Britons the other way if we were to air them.

This left me enough space to realise, somewhat awkwardly, that I have no desire to be British. I'm already French and Moroccan as it is, and getting a third nationality would feel greedy.

I am a Londoner, though, and that suits me just fine; I'd rather cross the Channel again than live anywhere outside the M25, and so getting a British passport would be cheating, wouldn't it?

What I am as well is a quiet immigrant, a foreigner hidden in plainsight: partly because of my much rehearsed accent without a trace of French, but also because of the privilege I was gifted along with my white face and middle-class upbringing.

In the time it took me to realise this, the UK had voted to leave the European Union. I had watched the night's result in shock, and couldn't help but sob when, walking home from a friend's flat at 6 a.m., I accidentally walked over a scratched 'Stronger In' sticker on the pavement.

The symbolism was quite heavy handed, but it's hard not to be a bit too earnest when you've had no sleep.

What followed was another epiphany – I am, it turns out, fiercely European. This was, again, not something I'd profoundly thought about before being made to, but my inadvertent reaction to the vote showed that my feelings were stronger than I'd assumed.

So where does that leave me? I've been here for too long not to feel alienated whenever I go back to France, I'm still too foreign to even think about calling myself British, and the one moniker which could suit me is the one my newfound home has decided to reject.

'So how do you feel about Brexit?' is a question I've heard far too many times, often followed by 'you know, given your status'.

'And how do you feel about the deal you're being offered? Are you staying here? How do your friends feel about it? How do you *really* feel?'

Unsure what to do with themselves, grief-stricken Europhiles decided at some point this year to turn us European immigrants into their figurehead.

They know that their fellow citizens voted against their wishes and there isn't much they can do about it, but can't they see those people, the ones who moved here in search of a better life, can't they see what they're doing to them?

We've been invited on television and on the radio, and nights have been organised in our honour, and everyone is now terribly concerned about what will happen to us, but really, I wish they weren't.

Being dragged into a culture war and paraded around as a living and breathing argument in favour of one side isn't, it turns out, particularly pleasant.

Brexit has been so omnipresent in my life and work for the past few months that it doesn't make sense any more; it's background noise which occasionally makes itself known when someone says something particularly stupid or offensive.

What this means in practice is that I'd rather not think about it, thank you very much – those who voted to leave clearly saw our implied relationship as too close for comfort, and those who wanted to remain mostly did for reasons that had nothing to do with us.

The deeper truth is also that I simply don't know where to stand. I am sad that you voted for what you saw as independence but I will probably stay here; I wish you hadn't voted the way you did but it wasn't about me and never will be.

Like the aunt quietly pouring herself more wine as the rest of the family drunkenly argues about politics at Christmas, I have no desire to get involved.

I have made my life in London and I am happy to have done so, but these existential convulsions of yours make me feel queasy, and I'd rather stay quiet.

My heart will always be European but don't worry; once you calm down and decide what and who you want to be, I'll still be here. At home.

CAVOLI RISCALDATI

(Reheated Cabbage. An Italian phrase that means
'the attempt to revive a failed relationship')

Holly McNish

HOLLIE McNISH has published three poetry collections, *Papers*, *Cherry Pie* and most recently *Plum* (Picador, 2017). Her poetic memoir of parenthood, *Nobody Told Me*, won the Ted Hughes Award 2016 and she co-wrote the play *Offside* with Sabrina Mahfouz. McNish tours the UK extensively, and her poetry videos have attracted millions of views worldwide. She has a keen interest in migration studies, infant health and language learning, and gives performances of her work for organisations as diverse as the *Economist*, MTV and UNICEF.

and she did not have *hairy armpits*
like my school friends all suggested
her white jeans not *our* fashion
nor her 'froggy' choker necklace

and her accent was not from *here*
and her English was not perfect
but it was a lot fucking better
than any language we had learnt yet

and she smiled and they stared back at her
spectators in our schoolyard zoo
elbowing each another, nudging
daring mortified 'Salut's

and they asked me if she smelt bad
and they scoffed up when she spoke
and they shuffled feet, silence
made more hand-hid jokes about her clothes

and I have never been so pissed off
at people by my side

as that day at school in year ten, when
my French exchange arrived

Two weeks I had spent welcomed
in a smaller town in Northern France
a moped under every kid
wine and beers and questions passed

her mates flocking over
to test the English they had learnt in class
everyone I met
two cheek kisses
and some nervous laughs

and I'm not saying
there is no prejudice
of course there's prejudice
in France

I'm just saying
that our prejudice
seemed steeped
in English arrogance
– and fear

Of languages, especially
the trying out of other sounds in mouth
The French kids quoted bands to me
Britpop lyrics muddled proud

Oasis versus Blur, *Le Beatles*
'Girls lick Boys' and 'Boys lick Girls'
but when the French kids came to England
we knew *nothing* of their world
we knew *nothing* of their pop tunes
of their singers or celebrities
we joked about their tastes
as if their culture stank of moulded cheese.

English radio does not play songs
which are not sung in English
Hardly any chance for many kids
to stumble on another language

Macarena filled my discos
and for a short time our tongues were tied
wobbling words excitedly
attempting unknown Spanish lines

but once in childhood's not enough
our island seemed so fucking closed
the day I stepped off of the ferry
and stumbled in her home

We soak influence across the globe
but only when it talks like us
America, Australia,
Caribbean at a push
US commerce lyrics
and films packed out of Hollywood

We were so petrified of oral
the most nerve-wracking of tests
those bitter school exams
not the licks between a woman's legs, tho

that is censored here as well
beside stiff happy cocks and breasts
I didn't know we were so shaded
until I watched a film in French

bodies not so airbrushed
nakedness that stood alone
in Hollywood I realised
naked bodies only groaned

skin stripped of all purpose
but the lustings of the flesh
I hadn't really thought outside before
British was the best

British was the marker
from politicians proudest mouths
spouting Britain's highest place
in every global league around

Education – best and Welfare – best
British working life
Our British health care system – best
I still think that one may be right

Goodbye Europe, fine!
it was a democratic vote
but I wonder sometimes what
if those childhoods weren't so closed

and I wonder now we're out
how the next kids in my town will think
how even less might learn a language
the effect that has on prejudice
how much more anglophone thoughts will be
how much more engrained that English pride
how much less we'll think that we might learn
from countries by our side

from Holland's sexual health
or Norway's reoffending rates
Denmark's Urban Planning
Of Sweden's paid parental leave

And it's not that we can't learn this all
without a European union
it's that I don't think kids will bother
cos I don't think culture here will push them

and now, I wonder how they'll treat them
if they can get here for those trips
or if some tighter visa system
will mean those French Exchanges quit

I wonder how the jokes
and how the welcome will be now
from a new young British school kid
in a Britain lone and proud.

A MIDSUMMER
NIGHT'S DREAM

Ece Temelkuran

ECE TEMELKURAN, one of Turkey's best-known novelists and political commentators, was a prominent investigative journalist before her controversial explorations of Kurdish and Armenian issues and her criticism of the current regime led to her dismissal. The author of the nonfiction works *Turkey: The Insane and the Melancholy* and *Deep Mountain: Across the Turkish-Armenian Divide* and fiction works *Women Who Blow On Knots* and *The Time of Mute Swans*, she has been a visiting fellow at Oxford and delivered the Freedom Lecture as a guest of Amnesty International and the Prince Claus Fund. She has contributed op-eds and articles to the *New York Times*, the *Guardian*, *Literary Hub*, and *Bookforum*. Her books have been published in nineteen countries. She lives in Istanbul and Zagreb.

Intellectual fashions are rarely mentioned in political history. So here's a helpful tip for future readers of this piece: nowadays almost every European media outlet mentions the fancy term 'rising populism'. The term somehow conceals the fact that Europe's mind is paralysed. The cacophony of identity politics, the weakening of political institutions that reduces democracy into a simple voting process, and the utilisation of democratic means by right-wing politics to mobilise the masses towards proud ignorance and self-evident provincialism, are overshadowed by the ongoing Syrian refugee crisis.

Looking at this picture from the periphery of Europe, it is as if a Trojan horse with banners of 'real people – real democracy' all over has just entered Europe after its long voyage in the rest of the world. It seems what has been experienced in Turkey for the last two decades to end up in an authoritarian regime is now coming towards Europe. This in fact is a phenomenon that might alter Hannah Arendt's 'banality of evil' to 'evil of banality'. The banal taking over the system of values established by philosophical and scientific improvement of last centuries to start is rite of passage for utmost political and social vulgarity.

One very telling, quick example of this 'evil of banality' is

Mayor of Ankara, Melih Gökçek, who was elected through the democratic process for four times in a row. The capital city of Turkey currently has one wristwatch and multiple Transformer-like and dinosaur statues. In neighbouring cities, people are even condemned to live with monuments of meatballs or watermelons. I leave the burden of imagining the political and intellectual environment where aesthetics is reduced to vegetable sculptures to the readers of these lines.

However, it is necessary to emphasise that when democracy is diminished to a simple voting process it takes a much shorter time than one might like to think for a country to find itself living the dream of ignorant masses led by psychotic leaders. The banal, and eventually the vulgar, legitimised by the democratic process, first imposes itself on the masses. Then, with limitless pride, it begins wiping off aesthetics, then critical thinking and finally stigmatises any deviation from ordinary as hostility against the 'real people'. A European might feel offended when such a similarity is drawn between a crazy Turkish mayor and European political sphere. Having seen both, unfortunately, they are brothers in banality, and evil is there waiting to acquire enough power to demonstrate its magnificence.

Despite hundreds of conferences and summits to discuss how Europe can overcome her philosophical and political fragility to keep its ideal intact in these interesting times, the continent not only as a region but also as an ideal is trying to isolate herself from the insanity that has been invading rest of the world. Although the isolationist politics become most visible when borders are closed to refugees, the more important matter is that the questions of our age are dealt with desperate practicality when fully formed philosophical responses are required. Stripping a woman from her burka by police forces on Cannes beach; leaving free-media/thought to deal with mercilessness of free-market economy through miserable financial support calls; desperate police effort to catch 'terrorists' when those individuals are clearly choosing new set of values over a European social security system embellished with supermarket fidelity cards ... These are all symptoms of the fact that Europe must renew its perception of the human being in order to deal with the questions of our age and to provide the masses with a new set of meanings against the tempting easiness of banality and politicised vindictive vulgarity.

In order to match the grandiosity of these questions, Europe as well should imagine itself bigger than the actual region and realise the fact that Europe is in fact a scattered continent. Today, even more passionately than in Paris or London, Europe lives on banners at Tahrir Square reading 'Dignity', in a teenager's angry diary entry about sexual equality in Islamabad or resistance graffiti at Gezi Park in Istanbul that reads 'We are Gandalf's soldiers'. I see it as a moral responsibility for European intellectuals to connect to the Europe that inhabits in the rest of the world and to think and speak together. Because Europe is still not as exhausted by the evil of banality as the rest of the Europeans in other parts of the globe. The Pantheon is not yet replaced with a French baguette and the Globe Theatre has not become the venue for pop idol competitions. It seems laughable, as the idea of meatball statues were hilarious to Turkish people once.

I grew up with sad stories of generations in Middle East countries that believed in Europe while Europe rejected them. They were stigmatised and excommunicated by the brutal backward masses in their home country while being alienated by Eurocentric thinking. In fact they were the Europeans living outside Europe, both capable of discussing Kant and criticising Eurocentrism. They were the ones who were trying to invent an intellectual space free of Occidentalism and Orientalism that can apply both to Orient and Occident.

Between 1940 and 1956, in the then young Republic of Turkey, intelligent but poor rural children were lucky enough to go to village institutes, where they had quality Western education to become teachers in remote towns to enlighten backwards Anatolia. Even today they are considered to be the best-educated generation of Turkey and their stories are told as an elegy to a dying dream for a better life. The famous old photo of the student playing Hamlet in some village square is still there to remind us what could have become of those scattered Europeans but, due to the global political history, did not. And today, generations of scattered Europeans are drifting with the storm while Europe herself is also losing her anchor.

Obviously, it has been a long while since I asked the question, so I had to go back to the mythology for the answer. What was happening to Europa after Zeus abducted her disguising himself as a white bull? She became a subdued housewife with kids in Crete. The question of our times is what would Europa's response be when she is once again bullied in the twenty-first century. The answer lies not in sedate lives in European capitals, nor in isolated European intellectual circles, but among Europeans scattered around the world who are experienced in the evil of banality but are too exhausted to solve the problem without the help of European intellectuals.

EUROPA

Chris Riddell

CHRIS RIDDELL is a renowned political cartoonist and the creator of an extraordinary range of books which have won awards including the UNESCO Prize, the Greenaway Medal and the Hay Festival Medal for Illustration. His work includes the highly acclaimed *Ottoline* titles and the 2013 Costa Children's Book Award-winning *Goth Girl and the Ghost of a Mouse*. Chris has also collaborated on books with high-profile figures such as Neil Gaiman, Roger McGough and Paul Stewart, and was Waterstones Children's Laureate 2015–2017. He lives and works in Brighton.

PARTY GOING

Olivia Laing

OLIVIA LAING is the author of *To the River*, *The Trip to Echo Spring* and *The Lonely City*. She writes for the *Guardian*, *frieze* and the *New York Times* among other publications. She'd like to stay in Europe, thanks.

I'm on the train from Rome to Trieste. Last night I had dinner next to three gossipy Irish priests in the Piazza Farnese. In the middle of the square there were two fountains made of vast marble bathtubs, taken by the Farnese family from the ancient baths at Caracalla. Everything in Rome is reused, repurposed. The priests were from Donegal. I bet I know at least one of them, John tells me from New York.

In another square, by another fountain, I watched a kind of hooded crow with a cape of pale feathers eviscerating a dead pigeon, flipping it to get purchase, tearing morsels of flesh, lordly as the diners at Ar Galletto. I noticed it mostly because I was reading *Party Going* by Henry Green, a 1939 novel in which a group of aristocratic English people on their way to a holiday in Europe are trapped in Victoria Station by thick fog. In the first sentence a dead pigeon falls from the sky. Miss Fellowes picks it up, takes it into the lavatory and washes it. Later she wraps it in brown paper and gives the parcel to a man to put in a bin; later still she retrieves it.

Hovering on the brink of Europe, trapped in a fog, unable to enter or retreat, the bloody old British. I see them here and wince: hesitant or bullying, overconfident, uncertain of their place.

The civic buildings give way to apartment blocks, peach and vanilla, rubble by the tracks. Europe is a boneyard, a dead land, stronger than ever, united, in tatters, at the end of its rope. Flying in yesterday, the dry summer landscape was scattered with chips of jade that grew bluer as we came down over Rome. The biggest was next to a field of ash. Tiny people sporting in the turquoise water.

Hard Brexit versus *la dolce vita*. This time last summer I was in Paris. I should have been in a gallery, a bar, but instead I was sitting on my bed, watching the news unfold on Twitter. Drunk English football fans in Lille, throwing coins at refugee children. Pictures of Nigel Farage with his sad beery smile, posing next to a truck displaying a photograph of young men in hoods and hats walking across a damp green landscape. *BREAKING POINT*, the caption said. And then an incident in the North. An MP has been shot and stabbed. The details are unclear. The man shouted something. The man shouted *Britain First*.

The next day was Bloomsday. We were at Shakespeare and Company, where for the past few years they've been conducting a Bloomsday reading of *Ulysses*, working their way inchingly through that rapturous voyage. I read after a flushed Irishman in a linen jacket. Leopold Bloom, the cosmopolitan, the wandering Jew. Funny how words have regained their malignant 1930s power, their covert racism, their false populist appeal. *Elite*, *metropolitan*, *liberal*, *enemy of the people*. At the end of that horrible summer Theresa May said: 'If you believe you're a citizen of the world, you're a citizen of nowhere.'

We didn't have to show our passports in Rome. We didn't belong to the Schengen zone, but we did have the luxury of free passage. I'd never been before but the architecture of the city was familiar to me from York, from Bath. We were always on the move; people, like the original Ulysses, of many turnings.

Outside, it's begun to rain. Little silver darts of water fly past the train window and vanish abruptly. I like it when we're different from each other. I feel safer, I feel richer. The illusion of national purity leads to trains across Europe packed with people who have been stripped of their possessions, clothes, children, teeth, humanity. Take back control: against what? People who want hospitals and schools, libraries, fresh tomatoes, an evening in the cinema.

While I was in Paris I took a screenshot of the Farage photo and saved it on my laptop. Looking at it again now, my eye is caught by a small boy. The crowd of walkers is ten deep, it snakes out of shot. I suppose you are meant to think that these men are coming for your wives, your daughters, that they are Muslims who will feast on Europe's plenty and then destroy it. This boy, this small Telemachus, has been caught in a posture familiar to anyone who has taken a long walk with a child: head thrown back, eyes closed, done in, over it, absolutely knackered. *We must break free of the*, the white text says, and then on the other side of Farage's shoulders, *back control of our borders*. I want to go home, Telemachus replies. I miss my mother, I miss my dog.

In *Party Going*, the fog stops all the trains from leaving. The group shelter in a hotel which soon locks its doors against the gathering hordes of travellers. Occasionally, one person or another wanders to the window to look out at the tired, jostling masses below. It is so pleasant to look down on a crowd, and then to shiver and return to one's tea. In the photograph Farage's shoes are very shiny. He trades in the same queasy fantasy of British exceptionalism and deserved privilege that Green is satirising. Outside the crowd keeps growing. They can't disperse. They have no choice but to wait there, on the edge of Europe.

It's nearly noon. I'm approaching my station. On the platform at Orvieto there's a monument carved with the words: *In memoria di tutti i ferrovieri caduti sul lavoro*. Travel exacts a toll and yet there will never be a day when we don't need to move, for love or water, away from bombs, looking for places of greater safety, of less peril, of more abundance. Wouldn't it be more civilised, more cosmopolitan to say yes, to unlock the doors, to pool the resources. *Yes I said yes*, the closing lines of *Ulysses*, and then the exile's small prayer: *Trieste-Zurich-Paris*.

SPEECH AT THE
CONVENTION ON BREXIT

Ian McEwan

IAN MCEWAN is a critically acclaimed author of short stories and novels for adults, as well as *The Daydreamer*, a children's novel illustrated by Anthony Browne. His first published work, a collection of short stories, *First Love, Last Rites*, won the Somerset Maugham Award. His novels include *The Child in Time*, which won the 1987 Whitbread Novel of the Year Award, *The Cement Garden, Enduring Love, Amsterdam*, which won the 1998 Booker Prize, *Atonement, Saturday, On Chesil Beach, Solar, Sweet Tooth, The Children Act*, and *Nutshell*, which was a Number One bestseller.

In the current state of Brexit politics, I belong to the smallest, saddest most pessimistic faction. I'm a denialist. Almost a year on, and I'm still shaking my head in disbelief – not a useful political act. I don't accept this near mystical, emotionally charged decision to leave the EU. I don't, I can't, believe it. I reject it.

My faction lives in daily bafflement. How has this happened in a mature parliamentary democracy, this rejection of common sense and good governance? How can it be that in a one-off vote, just over a third of the electorate has determined the fate of the nation for the next half-century? That shameless lies were told in the Brexit cause? That an advisory referendum has taken on a binding status? That politicians who spoke so recently for the EU now occupy the highest offices in the land and are driving us out? That a gang comprising many angry old men, irritable even in victory, are shaping the future of the country against the inclinations of its youth? That a handful of billionaires lavishly funded the Brexit campaigns for their own financial interests? That, in Guy Verhofstadt's words, a catfight within the Tory party got so completely out of hand? That the country, like a depressed teenage self-harmer, takes out a razor to scour a forearm, and now contemplates its own throat?

The Brexit constituency is a broad church. Take a look at the span. It contains on one wing its majority – many decent, concerned people who have made their own decisions derived from anxieties about immigration and the rapid changes it has brought to their localities; or they've suffered the harsher edges of globalisation; or they dream of what they think their country once was. Passing along the spectrum we come to what I would call the Anglican-Brexiters – Anglican because they are so close to the atheist Remainers one would hardly know the difference. They want a 'soft Brexit' – single market, customs union, free movement, European Court of Justice, big annual contributions – but no agency in shaping EU policy: utterly absurd. Why not be an atheist? Then we come to the current orthodoxy, the 'hard' caucus of economic suicides, of no customs union, no single market; they dream of instant, multiple trading treaties around the world whose arbitration clauses will miraculously not mandate courts higher than our own.

Moving along fractionally, we arrive among those who would have us 'crash out' of the EU without a deal. As we keep journeying, we find ourselves in the company of those who prefer Robespierre's grisly trope, 'enemies of the people', against any dissenting voices, and, of course, against the judiciary. Now we rub shoulders with those who stare out foreigners in the street, who, from behind the safety of their computer screens, have threatened rape and murder against Remainer activists like Gina Miller. Finally we arrive at the vilest manifestation, those who physically attack people in the street because they speak Polish, those driven by anti-immigrant passion to murder an asylum seeker in the peaceful town of Croydon, or murder a Labour MP because she was making the case for remain.

We find ourselves in a new country where it does not seem so very strange for a former leader of the Tory party to speak of war with Spain.

Truly, Brexit has stirred something not heroic or celebratory or generous in the nation, but instead has coaxed into the light from some dark, damp places the lowest human impulses, from the small-minded, the mean-spirited to the murderous.

For all that, the political energy and initiative has been with the Brexiters. What then of the Remainers? Hobbled by a fatal attraction to rational arguments rather than emotional appeals. We are a vast, peaceable crowd, 16.1 million strong, thoughtful, unhappy, leaderless, with meagre political representation. We don't threaten rape. As far as I'm aware, no Remainer has murdered a Brexiter. Our church, perhaps to its detriment, is not so broad. It is moody, tearful, complaining, sometimes cogently, even beautifully. In general, until now perhaps, it seems to have stoically accepted the process.

If the vote had gone the other way, by the same margin, the Leavers would not have crept away to confine themselves to soulful laments. They wouldn't be conceding that 'the people have spoken', that we must obey the command. No, they would fight on, just as they and their complicit, excitable newspapers have done for more than forty years since the last referendum. Didn't we hear Nigel Farage say there would have to be a second referendum if his side lost and the margin was narrow?

A second referendum on the terms of a bad deal, or no

deal at all is what we need to concentrate on. Therefore, take another look at Article 50. It's written in plain language. It's very short. It does not say – in fact it does not even address the matter – that once initiated by a nation, that nation must leave. We should borrow from Isaiah Berlin's concept of negative liberty and presume that in an open society, that which is not forbidden is permissible. I agree with the Brexiters who say that no deal is better than a bad deal. But that's not when we crash out and take our chances with punitive tariffs. That's when we crash in. And we don't even have to crash the EU party, because we are and will be already in it.

In this snap election, a progressive alliance is clearly beyond reach. Labour has preferred to go it alone. But in less than two years, a bad deal or no deal will be before us. Such an outcome deserves general scrutiny and general assent.

The complexities of a negotiated Brexit are already apparent; tempers on both sides are already frayed. For inherent, structural reasons, the trumpeted win-win arrangement might be beyond reach. By 2019 the country could be in a receptive mood and prepared to think again. Two and a half million over eighteens freshly franchised, mostly Remainers; one and a half million of my generation, mostly Brexiters, freshly in our graves. Set aside the negatives – rising inflation, lies about extra billions for the NHS, about 'hordes' of Turks, and so on. The EU, especially now with a Macron presidency, will be in the mood for reform and tighter Eurozone integration: a perfect moment to revive the plan for a two-speed Europe.

Many of us believe the EU remains the most extraordinary, ambitious, liberal political alliance in recorded history. It has overseen unprecedented peace and prosperity for seventy years. It is the dream trading bloc, to which we still have privileged access. Against the historical background of centuries of bloodshed, it is a heroic project, the closest embodiment on the planet of an open, free-thinking, tolerant polity forged between nations once at war. At the same time, it has preserved national differences – take a drive from Slovenia to Lisbon or Lubeck. At the human and cultural level, the EU is far richer, more diverse and benignly complex than continental USA. Where it needs reform, where it needs to evolve, we should be there to help turn that heavy wheel.

Developments these past twenty years have shown us that liberal democracy is not an inevitable development after all, but instead occupies a narrow bandwidth on the global political spectrum. And as the separate experiences of France, Britain, the USA, Poland and Hungary show, liberal democracy is frail, in need of constant renewal to ensure a more even distribution of the benefits. The EU project is under tremendous pressure: a hostile Russia, a less friendly USA, a migration crisis, irrational populist movements which offer opportunities to ambitious demagogues. Brexit will be a gruesome addition to these woes.

If Europe falls to the old, vicious nationalisms, history suggests that Britain will also suffer and be drawn into bloody entanglements as we have been so many times before. Good reason not to give up. It's a heartening feature of our civic society that so many groups are now taking up the fight – signing up younger voters, offering guidance on tactical voting – a great shame that the Labour Party will not lead the way on this. This is a parliamentary democracy. Our parliament, only recently so determined to remain, has let us down. Labour remains uselessly ambivalent. Too many Remainer Tory MPs prefer power and party cohesion to principle. The Liberal Democrats have been staunch but their base is tiny.

A pro-European civil society is now clearly ready to fight for what it believes. On 8 June, we hope for, and probably won't get, the sceptical, scrutinising parliament we should have. But by 2019, in the event of a crash-out deal or a terrible deal, we could have a sceptical electorate and a worried parliament amenable to pressure for a second-look referendum. Ignore the Brexiters who tell us daily that 'the people have spoken'. These are the same Brexiters who appear mortally afraid to let the people speak again. A negotiated settlement needs to be set before the nation for its consideration. If there's no deal, let's crash in, not out. Let the people speak – again!

This was a speech given at Central Hall, Westminster on 12 May 2017 to the Convention on Brexit.
(www.theconvention.co.uk)

STORM WARNING

Tom Bradby

TOM BRADBY is a novelist, screenwriter and journalist. He has written six acclaimed novels and numerous screenplays, including for the award-winning film adaptation of his first novel, *Shadow Dancer*, directed by Oscar winner James Marsh. Tom has worked for ITV for almost thirty years and is currently the Anchor of the channel's flagship news programme *News at Ten*, for which he has just won the award for Network Presenter of the Year. His work was seen by hundreds of millions all over the world when he conducted the engagement interview for Prince William and Catherine Middleton.

My most potent early memory of Europe is of the gulf which separates us.

I guess it must have been 1977, which would have made me ten years old. We were crossing the Channel in what I liked to tell people was a force 8 gale, but which, even allowing for a touch of inflation, I can still confidently say was bloody rough weather. In fact, the seas were so challenging that my mother (no slouch on a yacht) and a friend from school both retired to their bunks before we left the relative shelter of the Solent and did not emerge again until we were safely in the port of Saint-Malo.

You may very reasonably ask what on earth we were doing out there in such foul conditions, but my father was a naval officer, recently returned from a long spell at sea, who had also been the navigator for the 1964 America's Cup team. He could not conceive of any reason why inclement weather should get in the way of his holiday plans. He had every reason to think he could handle anything Neptune might throw at him, and I never once doubted that.

But boy, was it a long night.

It rained and rained and rained as we crashed through the violent swell with virtually no sail up in the howling wind.

337

Two hours out, my father offered me bangers and mash for dinner, and I nearly threw up at the very thought of it, let alone at the sight of him tucking heartily into his gourmet meal half an hour later.

Four or five hours beyond that, in the dead of night, he told me he needed an hour's kip. Keep the dots on the navigation dial together, he said, and wake me up if you see a supertanker. *A supertanker?* I couldn't even see my own hand. And as I sat in the soaked cockpit squinting at the dots on that dial and trying not to retch, I decided this is what hell must look like. I vowed never *ever* to go to the Continent again, or to set foot in a sailing boat.

Up until this point, the Channel had been a purely virtual gap, familiar from history lessons as the stretch of water that had kept both Napoleon and Hitler out. But after that night, with its visceral sense of just what a terrible place it can be, I looked at the waters between us in a new light, and it is something I have thought about often since. There *is* a reason we retain an island mentality. For good or ill, that stretch of inhospitable water is what sets us apart, both literally and metaphorically.

But equally memorable for me still is the dawn which followed that night from hell. Our arrival was delayed by the fact that the America's Cup navigator had left his glasses behind, and made an elementary error in the reading of his charts, to leave us a long way downwind of where we were supposed to strike land. But when I had got over wanting to push him over the side, I had to acknowledge what a glorious morning we had woken to. The storm had blown out and the skies cleared; a sunny fortnight on the beaches of Normandy and Brittany awaited us. Having become resigned to sitting in Fowey Harbour in the Cornish summer rain, I fell instantly in love. Everything about France seemed marvellous – the long lunches, the colourful cafes, even playing cricket on the beach with stale baguettes.

For us as a family there was no turning back after that. Europe beckoned. A few years later, my father was posted as the naval attaché to the British embassy in Bonn. We moved into a world immortalised by Le Carré's *A Small Town in Germany,* and extraordinarily civilised and comfortable it was too. Our new home was one of the fruits of West Germany's post-war economic boom. It boasted a boiler in the basement that could have powered a naval destroyer, and insulation – yes, *insulation*, a practically unheard of luxury in 1970s Britain – just about everywhere. It was so warm that I could wander around in a T-shirt in mid-winter, and, more familiar with a charming but draughty cottage in Hampshire and boarding schools that hadn't changed much since the eighteenth century, I was in heaven.

We took all our visitors on a tour of the local fairy-tale castles. We went cycling along the Rhine, *Sound of Music*-style, and eschewed afternoon tea in favour of the delights of *kaffee und kuchen*. Everything, from department stores to trains to restaurants, seemed that little bit more civilised than back home.

Best of all, though, was the close proximity of the *rest* of Europe, without ten-feet-high waves to separate us. We spent a lot of time on the *autobahn* bound for ski resorts, and the Austrian Alps remain to this day one of my favourite places on earth. I even thought about becoming a ski-racer for a while, and spent a lot of time training alongside young Austrian village kids who were half my age but had twice my talent.

My parents returned to the UK after a couple of years, but never entirely left Europe behind. In retirement they bought a house in France and I can still picture them, to this day, a few glasses of rosé down, making friends with their neighbours in their determined Franglais.

Meanwhile, I went into journalism and fell rapidly out of love with Europe, or at least with its politics. The Maastricht Treaty, the ERM, Brexit – on and on the arguments have tediously raged. After all these years, I am numbed by talk of it.

And through it all, I have often thought about my night on that inhospitable stretch of water, and of the land of *milch* and *miel* which then opened up so invitingly beyond it: our endlessly complex relationship with the Continent in a nutshell.

JAW JAW

Jenni Murray

One of my earliest memories is standing, aged three, holding my mother's hand, as we looked out of the bay window of my grandmother's bedroom. 'It was here,' she whispered, 'that I watched the Germans bombing Sheffield in the war. The sky was all red and I could see the flames as the city burned. And some of the bombs dropped not far from here.

'The Germans were off-loading what they had left on their way back to Germany. Mary Midgley had laid her wedding dress out on the spare bed, ready for getting married the next day. Their house was hit. Thankfully the family was in the Anderson shelter in their garden. The dress was blown to bits.'

For a baby boomer, born in 1950, the bitter wars that devastated Europe were only too real and 'the Jerries' were the baddies who featured in all our games in the street. My grandmother spoke of how the siblings in her family had been reduced from twelve children to eight. Four brothers had died in 1916 in the war to end all wars.

When I sneakily read my mother's teenage wartime diary, I found the details of several boyfriends whose names were crossed out. I didn't ask then, I shouldn't have been reading the diary, but I guessed what had been their fate. Years later she told me how many of her friends and 'beaux' had been lost in action in the Second World War. Dozens.

So, to my generation, the prospect of peace in Europe and an entente which would bring us together in a most cordial manner didn't seem to be about trade and economics, but a way to break down barriers and end the 'little England', 'Land of Hope and Glory' mentality which encouraged the Brit to consider him or herself superior to 'Johnny Foreigner'.

I was twenty-one when Britain went decimal – the first move towards parity with Europe. It wasn't easy. I first encountered the new currency when I returned from a year in France, required as part of my degree. The first thing I wanted to eat was fish and chips. I ordered and was puzzled when the bill was 50p rather than 10 bob. I passed over a handful of cash like a newly arrived stranger from a distant land. All rather odd, but a step in the right direction – towards a unified Europe.

It finally happened on 1 January 1973, not long before my twenty-third birthday. The *Guardian* wrote 'We're in . . . and a date which will be entered in the history books as long as histories are written, was taken by most people as a matter of course.' Two years later a referendum confirmed the majority of Britons wanted us to remain a member of European Community. There would be lots of 'jaw jaw' in Brussels and Strasbourg and no more 'war war'.

I could not have been more delighted. Future generations would not be blighted as our parents and grandparents had been. I had become a confirmed Francophile at school, thanks to the inspiring brilliance of Mme Short, my French teacher. She was a French woman who'd married an Englishman, looked like Juliette Gréco and swept into the classroom with the powerful scent of Worth's Je Reviens swirling around her.

She taught us to see lessons in speaking another language as a means of communication rather than the tedium of rote learning. I was deeply shocked to learn recently that her family had been known as 'the Froggies'. Not everyone in Barnsley was as keen on integration as I was.

I became a proud European, spending a great deal of time in France and Germany, adding German to my list of languages and cheering as the European Union grew and took on vitally important issues such as human, part-time and maternity rights and equal pay for work of equal value, changing UK law for the better, despite the frequent reluctance of national governments.

My most vivid memory of feeling thankful for being European came about during a visit to the theatre with some friends. I must have been in my early thirties and my companions were David, now my husband, Nancy, a friend from New York who was living in London and Uwe, her German banker boyfriend.

The play we saw was Bertolt Brecht's *The Resistible Rise of Arturo Ui*, subtitled 'A Parable Play' and written in 1941. It charts the rise of Hitler through the satirical story of an ambitious, fictional Chicago gangster who learns to speak effectively in public, goose step and make the notorious 'Heil Hitler' raised arm salute from a famous actor. He needs no training in how to use his 'boys' to bully his constituents into submission. The play ends with Ui on a high platform proclaiming his power to his public. The 'Actor' enters the stage to deliver the epilogue and speaks the chilling words: 'The bitch that bore him is in heat again.'

After the play, the four of us went to a pub for a drink. These two young men looked at each other and said what we'd watched must be seen in a strictly historical context. Yes, some forty years ago, they, an Englishman and a German, would have been trying to kill each other. 'But now,' they agreed, 'it simply couldn't happen. We're all Europeans now.' 'No more war, Tommy,' said Uwe with a smile. 'No more war, Jerry,' said David. And they hugged as if to underline the point.

I hadn't thought about that incident for a long time and, as the years have passed, we've gone our separate ways – Nancy to America and Uwe to Germany and David and I have raised two sons. They were both brought up as Europeans. They've travelled freely throughout Europe, learned the languages, enjoyed the reciprocal free healthcare and neither has so much as a hint of racism or xenophobia.

It was primarily for them that I wept when the result of the referendum was announced on 23 June 2016 and Brexit became the *mot du jour*. At the age of sixty-seven, I have enjoyed the best of the European Union already, but my sons are young with their lives ahead of them. That line 'the bitch that bore him is in heat again' keeps ringing in my ears as immigrants are demonised and 'make Great Britain great again' becomes a familiar mantra. The times feel frightening to anyone with a sense of history. I pray that Brecht's prediction was misguided, for the sake of the generations to come who deserve peace in Europe.

EYES OPEN,
MOUTH CLOSED

Georgia Donley

GEORGIA DONLEY is a GCSE student from Wiltshire whose favourite subject is English. She is very passionate about human rights, equality and animal rights. Georgia won the *Goodbye Europe* essay writing competition open to all UK based students aged over fourteen to be included as a contributor to this project with her piece *Eyes Open, Mouth Closed*. The prize was judged by Patrice Lawrence, author of *Orangeboy*, which won the Waterstones Children's Book Prize 2017, and *Indigo Donut*. Georgia hopes to go to university when she is older and she would like to be in a profession that helps people and makes a difference; perhaps a lawyer. She hopes to become part of the change she wants to see in the world.

These eyes are different to yours. These eyes have hope. These eyes are not fixed to stare endlessly at one idea, one view, one dream. These eyes gaze in wonder at the beauty of diversity and frown heavily at the narrow-minded nature that corrupts so many. These eyes watch the world differently; more forgivingly. These eyes watch as their fate is decided for them, they watch as politicians and preachers, speech givers and protesters fight without worthy reason. These eyes watched as their home began to change, began to shift. They watched as others more critical and angered with their own agendas and motives decided the future of these eyes. And I could do nothing . . .

Whether that is because a fifteen-year-old is considered too immature to handle big decisions, as lacking the knowledge and focus to understand what it means, nevertheless these eyes watched it happen. Even if these eyes did narrow at the sight of people dressed in fancy suits consumed by their own ego and thirst for power, nobody noticed and nobody cared. When they said 51.9 per cent of the British population voted, they meant the 'adults' did. Statistics from 2014 showed that 18.8 per cent of the British population were aged 0-15 years old. All those eyes that had to watch while their homes were twisted into propaganda, their parents growing more and more restless about their futures and people becoming angry and corrupted, completely self-assured that they were right. The conflict began to grow: wars were declared between parties forcing their fixed views onto the gullible minds spread across Britain, spending their days arguing about issues they clearly don't understand. These eyes watched as the tension travelling across the UK became a bigger focus than the decision itself; a decision that would determine *our* futures and *our* upbringings. And yet these eyes were still left watching. I couldn't say that we had been silenced by this issue because we were born into that silence; never being able to contribute a fragment to our shared community until strangers think we are ready to do so. These eyes are worthless to Britain while it remains caught under the heavy fire of ongoing battles for misunderstood terms and conditions.

Moreover, the referendum clutched on to the attention of every Briton for far too long; it can still be considered as a top priority now. Anything that can cause arguments and fallouts is worthy of the UK's concentration. Despite the final decision having been made through a democracy, it is obvious this wasn't an inclusive decision. These eyes watched on the side-lines as the rod was cast through our future pathways and possible choices. These eyes were never considered as anything other than soundproof windows built especially for preventing any reason coming through them; any speck of a chance to be involved in decisions that may reset any plans or ideas we had in mind. These eyes, like so many others, can do nothing but act as spectators arriving at an execution; having no voice or consideration, no hope or chance, no say or view.

It appears that, although having developed our technology, customs and ways of thinking, too much of the population remains forbidden to speak out. Ironically it seems, in that respect, human beings haven't evolved since 1868: a year that witnessed the last public execution in the UK, where civilians would observe, knowing they were completely powerless to stop it. These young eyes watched powerlessly, also, as Britain's fate was decided, for better or for worse, without many being able to provide their views. Perhaps this decision will be the execution of Britain as so many who decided were too concerned with prejudiced thoughts and grand speeches, that underneath contain no meaning, to actually perceive without corrupted eyes.

These eyes are wider than theirs; more optimistic and compassionate; more open to what others can offer. They see the world in a new way, granting their imagination complete control to guide them through the paths of others and build bridges that overcome the biggest of bigotry. Still, these eyes remain unappreciated. They are blanketed in the darkness by others who believe we are not ready to see the world for what it really is, not ready to wake from our dreams of equality and acceptance, to open our eyes to find a world far from peace and purity. But what those eyes don't see is the knowledge that these eyes have developed the understanding within that watches the world with both faith and awareness. These eyes are younger than yours, yes, but these eyes are not so adolescent that they cannot comprehend the daily issues faced. These eyes see what yours do, only they see the potential too; the possibilities of a situation rather than just the corruption and inability to change for the better. They don't just view a situation and tick a box stating there is no promise; no option to salvage or save or develop; these eyes look past the odds of failure. Unlike many that make up the British voters, I do not let arrogance or narrow-mindedness stir me to agree with the easy option – the damaging option. These eyes analyse the situation as a whole, regarding all outcomes. You may find this difficult to believe but these eyes hold the capacity for both intelligence and the ambition needed to make a supported resolution. Will age ever be disregarded by our peers due to their realisation of our usefulness and contribution? Perhaps they are too focused on stereotyping us as irresponsible children to notice our true potential and input.

Furthermore, because I wasn't granted permission to give my own input, I have been left apprehensive with situations around me, situations I had gotten so used to, changing. For the past few years, I have been lucky enough to go on family holidays to our own mobile home in France. One where I enjoy spending my time and look forward to crossing borders to get there. These eyes have grown to appreciate the beauties of places other than home and have adapted to feel comfortable going frequently. Unfortunately, due to the neglect many views have received regarding Britain's future, the decision to leave the EU has already started to negatively affect *my* livelihood. The results have meant the value of the pound already decreasing, and with my family paying an annual fee in euros, more money has been spent on the same luxury we paid less for previously. These eyes have seen the sudden, unnecessary changes brought by this decision. And now, a gift that brought my family happiness has been tainted by the greed and lust for power these eyes have witnessed through angered politicians and biased citizens.

Unlike many of these cynical minds making up the UK's voting population, these eyes look past gender and sexuality, faith and religion, ethnicity and race, and see other eyes; some more experienced and others unsure, many compassionate and lots blaming, but eyes nevertheless. Why is it that these eyes, along with many others who are more sympathetic and compliant, are left without a say, without a chance to contribute?

Unfortunately, it seems these eyes are to remain overlooked and invisible as long as there is an issue that creates an inconsistency in the future: our future. Too much of our population, parts with potential, will forever be abandoned in any future dispute that shudders Britain: a community slowly crumbling apart, breaking away piece by piece as new politicians slither their way into the minds of the British population, or the segment that has a say at least. Will these eyes ever be considered as a valuable contributor? Or will the younger generations be forced to suffer the aftermath of the poor decisions made by their 'superiors' forever more? Will they ever see the way these eyes do? I doubt it. After all, these eyes are different to yours.

FLIGHT PATHS

Robert Macfarlane

ROBERT MACFARLANE is the author of a number of award-winning and bestselling books about landscape, nature and 'the human heart', including *The Wild Places*, *The Old Ways*, *Landmarks* and *Holloway*. His work has been widely adapted for film and television, and translated into numerous European languages. He has also written films (most recently *Mountain*, which premiered at the Sydney Opera House) and the libretto for a jazz opera set in a former nuclear weapons test site. He is presently finishing *Underland*, about under-worlds real and mythical. He saw his first peregrine when he was six, and each winter he watches blizzards of snow buntings on the Cairngorm plateau.

This is a map, a map of birds, a map of the movement of the birds that bind us beyond borders, a map that unfolds in time each year.

January. Hard frosts in the fields of France, so lapwings have come to the Vale of Aylesbury; come in number, turning in flocks. Short days, milder air, snow thawing to bones on the fields. High piping peewit cries, and in the sunlight their spoony wings and fine crests are lustrous as oil, their chests ice-white. When spring comes some of these birds will move east and north-east, crossing the North Sea to the dwindling peat-bogs of Jutland, or to southern Norway where they will find their breeding grounds among red-boarded farmhouses, on low-lying fields, by glacier-smoothed backs of rock.

February. Big rollers bulling across the Bay of Biscay, born of a long Atlantic fetch. A guillemot rides them as if it were part of the wave, rising and falling with the swell, then diving a hundred feet down, two hundred, in search of food, forcing into the Bay's grey depths with those stubby wings, those stubby feet. A day later, a week later, it makes the long flight north to the island of Skokholm off the south-west tip of Wales, where dead heads of sea thrift thrum in the cliff-top wind, and the Rosslare ferries roll in the chop.

March. Cotton grass whitening fast on the upland moors of the Peak and the Dales. Bog asphodel starting to yellow, and the steady green glow of the sphagnum. Black eyes of little mires among the peat hags. Golden plovers – *Pluvialis apricaria*, the bird of rain and sun – are gathering here, arriving from Iberia, from the polders of the Netherlands, come up to their breeding grounds here on the heather and the hags. Metal-mottled, gold on bronze, and a cry that haunts the moor.

April. The cuckoo is back with its broad barred front and its Lego-yellow feet and eye-ring. Cuckoos in the willows of Wicken Fen, cuckoos among the coombs of Dartmoor, heard but hardly seen. Their flight path has brought them across murderous Malta to the ilex scrub of Provence, then – moving fast, north-north-east, thirty miles a day across France – over the Channel and into England for the middle of the month, some staying south but some flying further up, to reach the pine forests and birchwoods of northern Scotland by the first week of May.

May. Swifts, swifts, the swifts are here at last! Screaming in and round on banking turns, boy-racers burning up the circuit, shrieking crowds of crossbows, above school playgrounds and church spires and beer gardens, some of the last migrants back and some of the first to leave. They sleep on the wing, ascend to 600 metres or more at dusk, heading out over the North Sea on the glide, out beyond Stansted, avoiding the planes that are flying for Munich, for Paris, for Prague. Swifts are storm-seekers, moving ahead of thunderclouds where the updrafts drive insects to swift-height. Swifts are airscape-readers, flying round the southern edge of depressions to reach warmth where the insects will mass. When rain comes to the east of the country, the swifts make huge outwards loops across Europe in search of food: 2000-kilometre insect quests over Calais supermarket carparks, hot Belgian plains, the roof canopy of Paris . . .

June. Curlew lumbering into The Wash, heavy-bodied long-distance fliers, splashing down into the slip to rest and feed. They've come from the Lofotens in the Norwegian Arctic, from the Baltic coast of Sweden, from inland Finland. Shot at in France, shot at in Spain, safe in England. Almost a thousand birds on the mud, stalking steadily forwards, probing the slip with those long curved bills, letting loose their calls, setting spines shivering.

July. Swallows in pillboxes, barns, bothies and outhouses. Swallows on aerials, swallows on branches, swallows on telephone wires. Swallows skim-drinking from pond and lake and river, streamers flickering behind them, purple in the gloss of their feathers. Swallows fattening and feasting on flies, readying for their autumn journey: south to the Biscay coast, south to the Pyrenees, south-east along the northern edge of the mountain range, south into Spain and across the Mediterranean, south and on, to Namibia, to the Western Cape.

August. Ospreys beating south from Scotland on those great chessboard wings; two adults, three chicks. Keeping to the river valleys, using them as lines of navigation. A chick is killed on a high-voltage line. Across the Channel to Brittany for three weeks, hunting and strengthening there, then down over the Pyrenees to Extremadura in central Spain. Pause at the Rock, and then a night-crossing of the Straits to northern Africa. Thirteen steady days of flying over dry ground to Mali.

September. Apples are falling in the orchards of Sussex, Dorset and Hampshire. Apples are rotting and wasping in the long grass under the trees – and the reed-beds of the South Coast are loud with the last of the sedge warblers, bobbing on the feathery heads of the phragmites reeds, filling the air with their rambling song, as they ready for their vast journeys to the swamps of France, to the grasses of Spain, and on to their winter quarters south of the Sahara. The cold is coming and these little birds know it.

October. White-fronted geese, *Anser albifrons*, touching down in the Essex saltmarshes – the Blackwater, the Crouch, the maze of channels around Mersea Island – to the Severn Estuary, to the Swale Estuary. Burly birds of the north: bold black bars on the belly and a white hoop round the beak. They have come from Siberia, across Poland, the Baltic States, across Northern Germany and Denmark, across the Netherlands, and at last to their wintering grounds here on the mudflats of England.

November. Scandinavian goldcrests flitting from pine to pine in the forests of Sefton Sands, weathering out the worst of the winter on the Lancashire coast. Miniature punks with a spray-can stripe of orange down the centre of the scalp, picking moth eggs and spiders from nooks in the bark.

December. Long nights, short days, hard frosts. Up on the Cairngorm plateau: wind-sculpted dunes of hard snow, cold-shattered rocks and little sign of life except for the ptarmigan in their white winter plumage and the climbers in their bright-coloured jackets. A scatter of high cries on the northerly wind and suddenly in blows a blizzard of snow buntings – from Greenland, from Alaska, from Canada, from Finland, from Sweden – sixty birds, a hundred, moving as a single whirling turning flock in which it is impossible to distinguish origin from future, cause from consequence or individual from group.

We are related by birds.